Before & After

by

Tudor Robins

Tudor Robins
www.tudorrobins.com

Book Layout © 2017 BookDesignTemplates.com

Before & After / Tudor Robins -- 1st ed.
ISBN 978-1-9991338-3-2 (ebook)
ISBN 978-1-9991338-5-6 (paperback)

Other Books by Tudor Robins:

Island Series:

Six-Month Horse (Prequel)
Wednesday Riders (Book Two)
Join Up (Book Three)
Faults (Book Four)
Reason Why (Book Five)

Stonegate Series:

Objects in Mirror (Book One)
After Lucas (Book Two)
Throw Your Heart Over (Book Three)

Perryside Series:

Moving North (Book One)

Mystery Stables:

Stolen Saddles (Book One)

Stand-Alones:

Meant to Be (Young Adult)
Before & After (Women's Fiction)
In Search Of (Small-Town Romance)

Before

The two pictures say it all. Before and after.

Before there are eleven of us. Not a crease or a grass stain in sight. Every hair in place on every head. The flower girl and ring bearer smiling angelic smiles. Slightly blurry in the background and off to the side two of my aunt's near-black Canadians hitched to the wagon that brought the bride to the wedding.

Charlie and Bree are in the centre, of course. Stars of the show. Shining with anticipation ... and a few nerves.

On Bree's side Cleo and I smile, wide and genuine. Behind Cleo are Bree's parents – Cleo's grandparents – looking very similar to Charlie's parents on the other side; as though they're wearing waistbands that cinch and shoes that pinch. Standing unnaturally straight. If you look closely enough you can see the tan line Charlie's dad's baseball cap has left across his forehead.

On Charlie's side is his brother Sam who, truly, is always delighted with life, but looks even more so in the picture, and next to Sam is Dob.

Dob, who stole my heart in grade seven, then broke it at the end of grade eight when he told the rest of us he was going to the technical high school instead of the academic one Charlie and Bree and I went to. It was a pattern the two of us would stick to all through high school and after. Love, then hate. Happy, then sad. Together, then apart. But when that photo was taken, we'd been steadily together for a long time. We shared a too-hot-in-the-summer and too-cold-in-the-winter third-floor apartment. We had jobs and paid our rent. Charlie and Bree had asked us to be their best man and maid-of-honour.

When the wedding photographer jostled us into position for the Before picture I was positive I'd have a ring on my finger by the time she lined us up for the After.

In the After photo there are ten of us.

There are grass stains across the bottom of Bree's dress, and everybody looks a little rumpled. Cleo's updo is down. Both dads' suit jackets are unbuttoned. The flower girl and ring bearer have chocolate rings around their mouths and he's leaning on her, with her scowling at him. Charlie and Bree are beaming with relaxed happiness. Cleo and Sam have the look of people who've done their job well. My smile is tight, and my eyes are focused, not on the bride and groom, but on the space next to Sam where Dob should be.

But isn't.

Oh, and my ring finger is still bare.

Then, and now.

No ring, and no Dob since that day.

One

Buying the toilet paper is embarrassing.

I want to stick a sign on the package that says, I swear I'm not hoarding – I'm actually running low.

It's not strictly true, though.

I mean, it's not that I can't use it. I would definitely have put it on my shopping list in the next week.

Or two.

In the short seconds I spend playing "will-I-won't-I" in the narrow aisle of the grocery store, two people reach around me to grab twelve-packs, revealing a lot of empty space on the shelf behind them. That's it. I take one too.

Just one pack, mind. And only twelve rolls – no need for twenty-four.

A perfectly reasonable amount for one person, living alone. I dare anyone to think otherwise.

As the cashier scans it through, I push down my embarrassment with the thought of how much more embarrassing it would be if the doomsday scenario came to pass and I actually did run out of toilet paper having had this opportunity to bring home these, particular, twelve rolls.

That wouldn't be nice.

***

"Ho! Et tu, Aspen?"

Bree toes my shopping bag as she drops onto the bench across from me. My cheeks warm. "I just ..."

She throws her hands up. "I judge not. I have two Costco thirty-packs in the back of the truck."

"You don't ..."

"God, yeah." She holds up her fingers. "First, I live with two men, a teenage girl, and a kindergarten boy. People will try to tell you women are big TP users ..." She shakes her head. "... nuh-uh – when Charlie and Sam come in from a day in the fields ..."

I wrinkle my nose. "Info I do not need about your husband."

She laughs. "Second, it's Costco. The whole purpose of Costco is to buy in bulk."

I nod. Can't argue with that.

"And ..." Now it's her nose that wrinkles. "I mean, being caught without ..."

"I know, right? That was totally what pushed me to buy it."

She lifts her feet to the seat beside me, leans back, taps her head and says, "Great minds."

I place my feet on the seat beside her, and give my standard answer, "Like minds," and we both gaze out the window as the boat glides away from the dock.

We slip past the picturesque waterside campus of the National Military College, then pass Cedar Island, sporting one of Kingston's four red-roofed Cathcart Martello towers, and after that there's a straight view east along the St. Lawrence River, only recently free of ice, undeniably cold, and always beautiful to me.

As the ferry passes the first jutting point of the island, Bree stirs and sighs. "Any more insider info?"

"Why do you think I was buying toilet paper?"

"That's hardly insider info."

"John just sent a quick text. There's a cabinet meeting this afternoon. He said he'd send a better update after that."

"He still likes you so much."

Her words – the accuracy of them – hollow out my insides. John *does* like me. I sigh. "What is *wrong* with me?" I instantly regret saying it because this is not an opening Bree is shy to take.

She straightens, wriggles her bum back from the edge of the glossy, slippery plastic ferry bench and leans forward. "Well, since you ask ..."

I shake my head. "No."

"Yes, you did. You very much did."

Even though we haven't had this conversation for a while, I know exactly how it goes. She'll remind me Dob is a no-good cad, who ditched me at her altar, and ruined a lot of people's nights – including the bride and groom's wedding night – in the process. She'll tell me I don't owe him anything – certainly not my loyalty. She'll beg me to move on.

I don't think she's ever actually said, "You're not living your life," but that's what I hear whenever we go over this old ground.

Maybe she's as tired of that old lecture as I am, because she surprises me by saying, "Hmm ... let's see – you've met a super-smart, well-rounded, up-and-coming, deeply kind guy who is completely bilingual, looks equally great in a suit and running shorts, and will probably be the premier before the decade's out, adores you, and you don't want to drop everything to be the future first lady of the province – you're right, what's wrong with that?"

"I like the new material."

She gives her hand an airy wave. "If I want you to move on, I need to move on too. Out with the old, in with the new. Save my oxygen for John who, in all seriousness, *is* a pretty amazing guy."

"Yup." There's no argument to that. John is all the things Bree says he is. John is amazing.

The only fault I can find with John is that John is not Dob.

My turn to wriggle my bum back from the edge. "Well, it's definitely amazing to have John as an inside source."

Bree lifts her eyebrows with an "I-know-what-you're-doing" look, then obviously decides to let me change the topic. "I do, and don't, want to know."

"You and me both."

The tone of the engines shifts as the boat approaches the dock. Bree puts her feet on the floor. I put my phone away.

"Why don't you come over for dinner and you can tell us what you know by then?"

"Sure. Sounds good. Thanks."

We wait for the telltale lurch that reveals the captain-in-training is manning the bridge, then we both stand.

"Don't leave your toilet paper on the boat," Bree says.

***

A kiss on the cheek from Charlie. A hug from Bree, which turns into a group huddle as first five-year-old Bix, then Sam, join in. Guilty pleasures. I should be avoiding them.

When I sit at the table Checkers, the border collie, leans against my leg, licks my hand. "Checkers ..." Charlie warns, and the dog slinks away, but his affection may be the only kind I can accept for the next little while.

Cleo dashes in, rosy-cheeked, with hay in her hair, and manages to make both Bree and me trip over her as we serve the meal. "If you're going to be late for dinner, at least wash your hands in the powder room," Charlie growls as she shakes her clean hands in the kitchen sink.

"I'm not late, Dad. I'm just in time." She gives him a wink and slides into her seat a micro-second before I place her plate in front of her.

Dinner consists of far too much delicious food, constant chatter from Bix and Sam, and a long spell of silence as we all savour Bree's world-famous blueberry-peach pie made better – if possible – by generous scoops of French Vanilla ice cream melting into the pastry.

It's only after Charlie's brother Sam – older chronologically, but more like a big brother to Bix and Cleo due to a developmental delay he's had all his life – heads downstairs to his basement suite, and after Bix stalls his bedtime with half-a-dozen, "I-just-have-tos," and fourteen-year-old Cleo slips out into the dark to do night check on her small menagerie of alpacas, and pygmy goats, and pigs, and chickens, and rabbits, that Bree, Charlie, and I are able to sit around the long-planked dining room table, in the now-quiet house, and wrap our hands around steaming mugs of tea while I relay John's message to them.

"It's a good thing we bought toilet paper ..." I say.

Sitting with the two of them, I tell them almost everything John told me. We talk through it once, then again. Doing that thing human brains do – trying to make sense of something non-sensical.

"It feels like a dystopian movie," Charlie says for the third time. As though repeating it will make it more real.

To be fair, I read John's email hours ago, and it's still hard for me to believe it. To believe that today was a normal day. Kids were going to school. People were going to movies. Tonight, in bars in Kingston, university students will be pressing their bodies up against each other.

Tomorrow morning we'll wake up, and the Premier will hold an early morning press conference and he'll tell us we're in a state of emergency, and the schools, and movies, and bars will be closed. Pharmacies and grocery stores will stay open, but you can bet there won't be much toilet paper on the shelves.

And we're all supposed to "social distance." No more kisses or hugs from this second family of mine. Maybe no more dinners with them even. That one I'm not drilling down on yet.

"Is John sure?" Charlie asks, then shakes his head. "Of course he's sure – he's the media liaison for the Minister of Health."

At the door, as I toe my feet into my boots, Charlie's eyes have a glazed look and he's shaking his head. "Wow." He gives me another kiss on the cheek. I accept it.

"I'm going to walk to the end of the drive with Aspen," Bree says.

The door closes behind us and we're in the crisp night air, only a couple of degrees below zero, recrusting the puddles melted by today's warm sun, and that means it's perfect sugarbush weather.

"No sugarbushes this year, I guess," says Bree.

"Great minds," I tell her.

"Wow. Everything's changing, isn't it?"

She's right, and I'm still not sure she totally gets it. Or I totally get it. It's one thing to say everything's changing – it's another to face it day by day.

She stops in her tracks. "What about your March Break bookings?"

I have two families due to arrive Saturday – one booking into the loft apartment over the barn and the other in the small cabin at the edge of the woodlot. Between the week's accommodations, and the extras they'd pay for while they were here – some packed lunches, maybe a barbecue dinner, wagon rides behind Campbell, and the extras Cleo offers my guests: alpaca walking, pygmy-goat petting, and fresh eggs from her hens – I was looking at thousands of dollars.

I was looking at paying off my interim tax bill with the proceeds.

"Um, yeah, if the families don't cancel tomorrow, I'll have to do it."

"But ... can you at least keep the deposit?" Bree knows how important that income boost is to my just-scrape-by existence.

"I don't think so. I wouldn't feel right about it. This is ... I guess ... the closest thing to an act of god, or a war, that we've experienced in our lifetimes. The usual rules don't apply."

"Oh, Aspen ..."

Bree knows there was a time after I inherited the farm from my aunt – after the elation wore off and I realized everything needed to be repaired and there were years of back taxes owing – that I was afraid I wouldn't be able to keep it. She knows how much I'd love to stop supply teaching – responding to 6:00 a.m. phone calls, rushing to get the horses taken care of and myself presentable in time to catch the next ferry, then showing up in classrooms where the students think supply teachers are for ignoring, or cursing out, or throwing things at.

It's not always like that. Lots of schools are nice, and lots of kids are sweet. Sometimes I get repeat gigs, which means sometimes I can plan my mornings.

But Bree knows I'd like to make the farm pay for itself. That I'd like to cut down on, and eventually stop supply teaching.

This pandemic thing could really throw a wrench into my plans.

Not only mine, though. Nobody's going to come out of this untouched, and at least I'm in a place I love with people I love.

"I'll figure it out." I hug Bree – the social distancing measures aren't official yet – and say, "Now go home and talk to Charlie. I think his mind is more than a little blown."

The full moon showers light on my best friend's slight form as she strides back toward her house well-equipped with toilet paper and love.

When I can no longer hear the crunch of her boots on the gravel, I turn down the drive toward my own house. Although we're officially next-door neighbours, this time of year the field between us is too muddy to cross and we have to walk the long way round; by the road. Which is fine with me. It lets me confirm that the fields are quiet. It gives me a chance to snap a shot of the barn, silhouetted by the crazy-bright moon.

It's been a while. I've been strong. But news like I've had today would wear down anyone's resistance.

I press the buttons I need to caption my photo **Home**.

It's not that I don't want to ask, *Where in the world are you?* It's that this is where we're at. This is the stage we've reached in our slow clawing back from ... well, from his complete abandonment of me at my best friend's wedding.

I've often thought this process I'm going through with Dob is akin to the stages of grief – it's just that I don't seem to go through them in any neat, tidy, or methodical way.

Asking too much – knowing too much – could easily tip me into a stage I'd like a lot less than the one I'm in now, so ever since he reached out to me following my aunt's death, we've stuck to being polite and remote.

I know he's alive. He knows I am. Good enough.

Can that be good enough when the world's turned upside-down, though? Can this entente between Dob and me really be the only thing in this world untouched by the virus? I'm fighting the urge to ask, *Are you in China? France? The UK, or the US? Please say you're not in Italy. Please.* I press send on the photo before I can type any of those things, then I send a silent apology to Bree – *Sorry, I'm not quite ready to move on.*

I rationalize it by thinking if this correspondence with Dob comes to nothing, Bree never needs to know about it. And if my wildest dreams come true, and Dob and I reconcile, and live happily ever after, then Bree will be happy for me, because that's what best friends do.

As I push the door into the warmth of the house, my phone pings, and I'm instantly as short of breath as if the dreaded virus has hit me.

I have to dig the phone out of layers. Have to swipe and swipe again with my cold, cold fingers to get to the notification.

John.

Oh.

John: What a day. Wish I hadn't had to send you such overwhelming news.

Me: No – it was fine. It's good to know ahead of time. Thanks to your heads up I got lots of toilet paper! (Joking. Sort of.) Please take care of yourself.

Then I resist the urge to listen to the news, and go to bed.

Two

The press conference is scheduled for early. Before most people are in the office. When many of them will be eating breakfast in their kitchens, or listening to the radio on their way to work.

So as many as possible of them will hear. So they'll know not to drop their kids off at daycares they'll need to turn around and go right back to.

I'm looking after my own children.

Four-legged, with shaggy coats coming out in clumps as the winter draws to an end.

I've kicked them out, where they stand tugging hay from the slow feeders in the paddock, shifting their backsides around in a quest to catch the earliest rays of the sun, and I've cranked the radio volume so I can hear it over my usual morning stall-mucking soundtrack of pick, pitch, and pad.

The Premier never speaks on time. Pundits fill the airwaves with speculation about what he'll say. They're touching on a lot of the points John sent me. With news this radical no doubt the leaks were strategic, to let the details float out, to keep them from completely shocking everyone in the province.

I've finished Mocha's (Salted Caramel Mocha) stall and have moved onto Lemon's (Lemon Sunshine) by the time the broadcasters all hush and shush each other, and the Premier begins speaking.

"My friends ..." he says. He's the king of the shit sandwich. Start with something nice, fill the middle with things we don't want to hear, end with something nice.

The filling is definitely unpalatable. Schools closed. All of them. Bars, nightclubs, indoor recreation facilities ... closed. Restaurants open if they can provide take-out or delivery. Otherwise – you guessed it – closed. Pharmacies and grocery stores are open, but for the love of God, don't hoard toilet paper. I choke, drop a pitchfork of manure back into the almost-clean stall I'm working on, then recover in time to hear him emphasize: Wash your hands. Stay two metres away from other people. Wash your hands. Don't touch your face. Wash your hands.

And, in conclusion, "... we'll all get through this together, my friends."

Before I can really think about what I've heard – before it can fully sink in that John had it all right, and everything's different – there's a squeal from outside. I prop my fork against the wall and step out to find my aunt's sweet Canadian broodmare, Campbell, standing in the middle of a running, bucking, maelstrom of activity which likely started with the two Morgan mares, Lemon and Mocha, chasing Campbell's three-year-old colt, Abbot, but has turned into a kind of whirlpool of hooves, and teeth, and tossing heads, and bannered tails, as the three of them buck and fart in a circle with Campbell at the centre.

When she sees me, Campbell lifts her head and whinnies. I lean on the fence, "You poor girl – are they all crazy?"

She stretches her head out and walks toward me, and even in their frenzy the younger horses retain sufficient sense to give her a wide berth. She may be sweet, but she's also their boss, and she won't hesitate to remind them of that if she needs to.

When she reaches me, Campbell props her chin on my shoulder and gives a long whiffling exhale and I thank everything I've got for the horses in my life.

***

As I sit at my kitchen table, with a slash of sunshine slicing across my laptop, and a steaming drink beside me, I think in many ways my life won't change. I'll still work on my own acreage. I'll still talk more to horses than to people on any given day. This is how my non-supply teaching days tend to go.

Except, of course, there's the undoing of the small-but-vital stream of income I've spent two years of word-of-mouth establishing.

If I hadn't had to feed the horses and try to keep the farm I would never have had the guts to go out on a limb and offer vacation rentals. On the "fake it 'til you make it" scale, I'm still firmly faking it. I wonder if I'll muster the courage to build the business up for a second time?

I log onto my vacation rental website and make sure I have bookings enabled through the entire next calendar year. Then I send a bulk email to everybody with a reservation for the next eight weeks. **Due to the state of emergency just declared in the province, I am currently canceling all bookings until late spring. For those of you who would like to re-book later, please use the code "pandemic" to receive ten per cent off your booking.**

Then I email the two families set to arrive the day after tomorrow, with a more personal message, offering them first dibs on next year's March Break, with the same enticement of a ten per cent discount.

Then I add up the amount of business I just canceled, chew on my pen, and try to figure out how to make some of that money back in the meantime while everything around me is shutting down.

Shit.

I push back on my quickened breathing, and my elevated heart rate. *Other people have bigger problems. Don't worry about things that are out of your control.*

But I'm human. So I worry.

I also know the solution to my worrying lies with non-humans. So I go out to the horses.

Lemon and Mocha aren't mine. They belong to a lovely woman who spends six months of every year in an ex-pat community in Mexico and likes coming home to the warm weather, and two eventing-ready horses.

With borders closing all over the world, I have no idea when she'll make it back from Mexico. I have no idea if there will be an eventing season this year. But I do know she's already paid for this month's board, and since this is the month I always start conditioning her horses, the payment was extra to include the time I'll spend working with them, and for the farrier to put their shoes back on, so Lemon and Mocha are getting conditioned whether they see a cross-country course this season, or not.

* * *

The world around me might be grinding to a halt, but tomorrow is the first day of spring, and it's as though my surroundings are saying, "Hey, look – you may have forgotten, but this is what spring is like!" The sounds are of singing birds, running water – everywhere, rivulets running through ditches, under the remaining snow pack, and when we ride along the shore, in the bay, finally free of the winter ice – and a light breeze, as opposed to a winter wind, in my ears.

There's also the crunch, crunch of hooves – both Mocha's and Abbott who's ponying along with us so I can get some fitness into him as well.

The strength of the sun is noticeable, and whenever we turn just the right way, and it beats down on us while the breeze retreats, I can feel it right through to my bones.

I always used to be an OTTB person, but these Morgans have won me over. They're strong, smart, full of personality, and they love working. Mocha's ears are short and curved, and nearly meet at the tips as she surges forward in her swinging walk, and her attitude is a big part of the reason I like to pony Abbott with her. He's three – the last of my aunt's homebred Canadians – inherited from her along with the farm – and as I prepare him for saddle work, my aim is to produce a horse who loves work as much as his stable mates do.

We make a big loop into Charlie and Bree's enormous acreage, then around the edge of my small property, past all the parts that are so precious to me. The big field separating my house from Charlie and Bree's where, before he and Bree bought their most recent hundred acres, and Bree decided it would be nice to have grass instead of corn in front of her house, Charlie used to grow crops and share half the profit with my aunt.

The woodlot, stretching behind both our houses all the way to where the land breaks away at the precipice tumbling down to the wide river, where Bree and I used to wander the foot worn trails. As young kids, we spent hours building forts under the trees and finding treasures – pine cones, trilliums, acorns – to adorn them with, until my Aunt Jean would come to the edge of the woods and yell, "Gi-ruls! Dinner time!"

As teenagers we'd walk through at twilight scaring ourselves on purpose – "Did you hear that? Somebody's following us ...", loving the quickening of our pulses and the goosebumps rising on our skin.

Later, when Cleo was a toddler, we'd bring her with us, boosting her up to climb the same trees we did when we were her age.

And, after Dob ghosted me, and I bounced around between denial, and anger, and bargaining, I might have gone crazy if I hadn't been able to walk the woods and the river.

Over the last couple of seasons, I've built cross-country fences across those old footpaths, and when they're jumping fit, I ride the horses through regularly to make sure they'll attack anything on any eventing course they're faced with. It's one of the reasons Agatha boards her horses with me – "When they've been with you they never refuse a fence, and they never run out of steam, and that's all I ask for," she told me when she bought Lemon last year and sent her to me.

Today Mocha, and Abbott, and I go all the way down the road to the edge of the property where we turn down the fence line and follow it to the shore. From here I can turn and look at the wide sweep of the property I love so much.

It wasn't long after Dob left that my aunt got sick. I instantly gave notice on the apartment I no longer shared with him and moved back here to help her and, eventually, to look after her. "Such a sacrifice for you to make," people used to say. "Your aunt is lucky she has you."

The truth was so different, though. My aunt, and this land, saved me twice – first, when all my mom's vices caught up with her, and she could no longer provide me with any kind of safe or healthy life, and a second time when Dob's disappearing act stripped me of all my confidence and security.

I have to hang onto this place. Just the thought of losing it drops the bottom out of my stomach.

I turn Mocha back toward the barn and resist the urge to open her up into a headlong gallop. Far from chasing all my troubles away, if she put her leg down a groundhog hole, or strained a still-unconditioned muscle, I'd be risking the board Agatha pays, like clockwork, every month.

Today, more than yesterday, I really can't afford that.

***

Come for dinner? Bree's text buzzes in as I'm looking through my cupboards, feeling hugely uninspired.

Probably shouldn't. Social distancing.

The phone rings before I can set it down. "No, no, no."

"Hi, Bree."

She ignores me. "Have you seen anyone since you saw us last night?"

I think of the faces of my four horses, and of the sweet mom from the family who now won't be coming to stay, who video-chatted with me, assuring me they'll come next March Break, if not sooner. "Not in real life. Not a human."

"So, what's changed? You were here last night. You can come here tonight. I'm not letting you spend the next fourteen days – or however long this goes on – completely alone."

"You can't pull me into your family just because you feel sorry for me. I'll survive."

"Yeah? Well I might not. Without you I'm living with Charlie, and Sam, and Cleo, and Bix. All of them dumping stinky clothes in my mud room all day long, two of whom pee on the back of the toilet rim."

"Hmm ... yes, well, I don't pee on the back of the toilet rim."

"See? I need you in my life. Come over usual time."

Even though the snow's rapidly evaporating, and the full mud of spring hasn't set in, I don't try my luck cutting across the field to Bree and Charlie's.

Halfway down their long driveway, I meet Cleo with her pygmy goats on their leads. "Keeping their manners up to scratch?"

She sighs. "Well, yes, but I'm not sure why. Bree said you had to cancel all your bookings?" Other people get confused when Cleo says "Bree" instead of "Mom" but I get it. It was never a secret that Cleo was Bree's daughter, but Bree's parents refused to let her drop out of school. Until Bree was done university, they mostly raised Cleo, which is why Cleo calls her grandmother, "Mama" and her mom, "Bree" and, just to confuse things, she calls her father "Pop," and her grandfather "Poppy" and it's all clear to me, because they really are the closest thing I have to my own family.

"More like postponing them," I tell Cleo. "I'm offering a discount code for them to re-book later, so I'm sure there will be lots of people staying and they'll all want to see your animals." Faking confidence for Cleo is good for me. I'm suddenly imagining my properties booked as far as the eye can see after all this is over.

The little goats crowd around my feet and nibble my fingers. Even though I can see them any day of the week, it still sends a thrill through me to feel their velvety noses pressed into my palms. I can understand why the people who stay with me think it's such a treat to book "playtime with the goats."

I snap my fingers. "Hey, since you have all this extra time on your hands, maybe you could make up a brochure I could give to my guests. That would probably get you even more bookings."

She tilts her head. "Yeah. OK. Not a bad idea. I mean, what do I have to lose, anyway?"

We stroll toward the house at pygmy-goat-pace – which is to say, starting and stopping fairly often, and Cleo says, "You know, I don't mind missing school ..."

I push down a smile at what's probably the understatement of the century. Cleo doesn't go to parties, or go shopping. She borrows, buys, and rescues animals, then more animals, then she trains her animals. Her entire social media feed is her animals. The only time she enjoys leaving the island is to take one or the other of her animals to 4H competitions.

"... what really bums me out is our 4H club just kickstarted that fundraiser to go to the Provincial Winter

Fair in the fall – assuming there will even *be* a Winter Fair in the fall – and now a bunch of the activities we were going to do to raise money will be canceled."

"I know Cleo. I'm sorry."

She meets my eyes, and sunshine spreads across her face, and this is Cleo – this is the charm she carries with her, and can turn on in an instant. She twirls around and the goats follow her in a capraesque dance. "At least I'm quarantined with everything I love. There are a bunch of girls from my class who will be going through vape, and eboy, and shopping mall withdrawal."

I wink. "Wise words, indeed."

Bree cranks the kitchen window open and yells, "Dinner!" and, like Cleo, I focus on thinking about the reasons I have to be grateful. After lasagna, and while we're waiting for Bree to spoon out ice cream for dessert Bix asks, "So – are we living in the middle of history?"

We all take turns telling him about other big things we remember that have also been written into history – the ice storm of '98 that hit the island particularly hard, with power out for three weeks, the 2003 Northeast power outage that led to a surge in the birth rate nine months later, and, of course, 9/11 – but we all agree there's nothing that's felt quite like this to any of us.

Charlie winks at him. "You're going to look back on this and remember how awesome it was that you had weeks and weeks to hang out with nobody but your family."

"And Aspen, too," Bix says.

Bree pauses in the middle of collecting dirty dessert plates to say, "Aspen *is* our family."

Bix shrugs. "I mean, yeah, I know, but why don't you have your own family, Aspen? How come you're not married?"

My eyes fly to Bree, and I catch her eyes as they flit to the before-and-after wedding photos she keeps in a cluster of other family photos, then back to me.

I wish I could laugh and tell Bix – "I haven't met the right person yet," – but Dob is the one thing in my life I'm no good at shrugging off, so I stay frozen, with my mouth open, and no answer at all for the five-year-old's question.

Cleo jumps in and says, "Women are *way* better off not getting married, Bix."

And Sam follows up. "We don't want Aspen to get married, Bix. Then she wouldn't come here for dinner all the time."

My chest tightens and my eyes water, and it's not because I'm still hung up on a guy who left me without a backward glance five years ago, or because the world as we all know it is turned completely upside-down; it's the sincerity of what Sam just said, and the big, sweet smile he's giving me.

Bree catches me blinking and leaps in, "OK! We're farmers! Even when the rest of the world has been thrown out of their routine, we stick to early-to-bed and early-to-rise, and there's no way you're going to get to bed on time, Mr. Bix, so let's go!"

* * *

Bree walks me home again. "I'm sorry about Bix."

"Nuh-uh – no apologies for Bix. Bix is direct. That's probably a good thing."

"Well, since my direct kid opened a great big can of worms ..."

"Are you calling Dob a worm?" It's weird to say his name out loud.

"More like a snake."

"Wait a minute ... weren't you the one telling me to get over him?"

She snorts. "Yes. And I stand by that. *You* need to forget all about him. *I'm* going to harbour a tiny grudge against him for the rest of my life for walking out on two of the most important people in my life. He didn't just abandon my best friend; he turned his back on my husband. He was supposed to be his *best man*. And he chose my wedding ..." She stops, shakes her head. "Sorry. We might have covered this before."

"You think?"

Dob did a spectacular job of ruining Bree and Charlie's wedding night. On an island, close to the water, when people have been drinking, there's very real reason to worry if somebody who should definitely be at a certain place, at a certain time isn't there. And still isn't anywhere to be found an hour later. And an hour after that.

That night I struggled out of my bridesmaid's dress and tugged on a borrowed pair of Bree's track pants. While a selection of relatively sober men scrambled down the steep bluff face, and searched the rocky shore at the bottom, Sam and I took an industrial flashlight, and Checkers, with us to the duck pond on the edge of my aunt's property.

By the time we got back it was 2:30 a.m., and the best any of us could say was we hadn't found Dob's drowned body. Bree, who was supposed to be in the honeymoon suite of a very posh inn on the mainland, was making tea and coffee and had called the ferry captain who polled the crew. Nobody had seen Dob, but that only meant he hadn't been in any of the public parts of the boat; hadn't crossed paths with any crew members.

The ferry was berthed for the night, and the provincial police weren't prepared to mount a middle-of-the-night search for a grown man who'd only been out of sight for a few hours, so the wedding ended with a group of

TUDOR ROBINS

people, bleary-eyed for all the wrong reasons, making
their way home or finding places to collapse in Charlie
and Bree's house.

"It's funny," Bree says. "But with everything that's
happening now, that night keeps coming into my head. I
think it was the radical change in plans, and the having-
to-make-do, and also – and I'd never admit this to Dob –
there was a silver lining in the sense of community that
was quite comforting. So many people working together.
You know, whenever I see anybody who went out looking
that night, there's a warm feeling in the pit of my
stomach."

I nod. "I know what you mean. Sam was a star that
night."

Bree sniffs. "Oh, you're making me all emotional."

"It's possible that living in a pandemic, having had a
glass of wine, and being out past your bedtime could be
doing that."

She swipes at her eyes, then flutters her hands in the
air. "When did you get so wise?"

"I'm intensely wise about other people's business."

I'm also very glad we've veered off the topic of Dob,
because that's where my wisdom falls down.

My brain knows he abandoned, not only me, but
everybody in the most disruptive and self-centred way
possible.

• 36 •

It knows there's no good explanation.

It knows I'm better off without him.

But my heart ... well my heart has an unhealthy obsession with Jane Austen, where cads can be misunderstood, and people can be destined for each other, and bumps along the road are there to make the ultimate love story more interesting.

I'd probably be far better off if I'd never read Pride and Prejudice.

I probably wouldn't have sent that text last night. I probably wouldn't have replied when Dob broke his years-long silence back when my aunt died.

"You look sad." Bree tugs at my sleeve. "Why don't you come back and sleep at our place? Bix will share his buttermilk pancakes with you in the morning."

I smile. "You think I look sad because you feel sad. It's a classic case of transference. Trust me – I know – a wise person recently told me I'm wise. And, anyway ... horses, night check ..."

"You sure?"

"Very sure."

My certainty wobbles when Bree turns back to her house, but I remind myself of the time Lemon figured out how to open her stall door, then went around and opened all the other stalls, and I stepped into the barn to find the horses very much not social distancing, so I really do need to do that final check.

Fortunately, everything's quiet tonight.

I glance in the barn, where the dozing horses are giving off enough body heat to keep the temperature somewhere above zero, and they're all content, and cozy, and they don't know there's a pandemic sweeping the world, and I wish I didn't have to know either, and I allow a tiny rush of fear to spike in me, followed by a fleeting surge of self-pity – just enough to make my eyes well – at which point I bite my lip; tears will require me to touch my face, and we can't have that.

Campbell's hung her big head over the stall door, and I wander over to tug on first her forelock, then her droopy lip. I rub the whorl of hair in the middle of her face and whisper, "Who's my best girl?"

Which is when my phone pings.

Even in a pandemic, technology will hunt you down.

I slip Campbell a carrot, which leads to whickering and agitation from the other three, so I hand out a bunch more carrots, then make sure the barn door latches behind me as I head back to the house.

The notification was from my vacation rental app, letting me know somebody, somewhere out in the big, wide, virus-ridden world, has made a booking.

I *knew* my ten per cent discount offer was a good idea. I click my laptop to life to see which of my displaced clients has re-booked for next year, and I stop and stare.

Shit.

The booking is for tomorrow.

"No, no, no ..." After I canceled the March Break bookings, it never occurred to me to block that time off. I mean, the world's in lockdown. Who's browsing for vacation rental bookings right now?

Dan Summer. That's who.

And he wants to stay for fourteen days. I look at the total charge and start imagining using it to pay my taxes, then I shake my head. He probably meant to book for next year.

I click on the email address he's provided and type out a message. **Dear Mr. Summer, Thank you for your interest in my vacation rental. At the moment you've selected arrival tomorrow for a fourteen-day stay. I suspect, perhaps, you intended to book for this time next year? If so, I can easily move the reservation for you and I'll be happy to welcome you next year.**

Then I flick on the ten o'clock news while I do a final tidy of the kitchen.

Every story is about people trying to get home from all different parts of the world. It seems like this virus has sparked a longing in people to figure out where they belong, and who they belong with, and to make it happen. I hear about a woman falling to her knees with gratitude in Pearson airport. A Canadian-American couple abandoning their year-long wedding plans and getting hitched in a registry office to make sure they can weather the pandemic together. A psychologist talking about how who we go into lockdown with is as important for our mental health as where we go into lockdown is for our physical health.

If I hadn't just had dinner with my favourite people in the world, I might feel a flare of self-pity for living here alone, but I make a concerted effort to count my blessings for being in my home, with my horses right across the yard.

I think of all the ways I could be worse off, and all the people stuck in far-flung places who must wish they could kiss the floor at Pearson.

I try, very hard, not to think of Dob.

It's not really working so I shut off the radio and go to bed.

Three

As I wash my breakfast dishes it becomes apparent that following the news is not going to be good for my mental health. I listen to the governor of New York say the virus is descending on his state like a bullet train. I look out my kitchen window, across the river to New York State.

A psychologist is interviewed saying our society is collectively experiencing the five stages of grief and it might take us a while to get out of the denial stage. I don't need anybody else to teach me about denial.

I flick the radio off and go outside to do turn-out and clean the barn, then work with Abbott.

I talk to him as I groom him. I always talk to my horses. I tell him it's almost go time. "I checked and the snow's gone from the shed doors." I run the jelly scrubber over his muscled rump. "We can open them. We can get Aunt Jean's wagon out."

I take a step back and notice how much sleeker his black coat looks even since last week at this time. "You're getting so smart, and strong – now we need to put everything you know together." Then I give him a final scratch on the withers before I go to get his bridle and the long lines. "You were bred for this."

**

The snow's gone from the sand ring, but it needs a couple of solid days of island wind and sun for the footing to dry out and be really usable. That's OK, though, because Abbott and I are fine using the driveway.

The months of groundwork, liberty work, and voice training I've been doing with him are paying off as he moves easily ahead of me. He's not completely confident all the time, but he has stretches of confidence, and when it falters, he flicks an ear to me, and I give him the support of my voice or my hand.

At the top of the drive I look across and see Charlie pulling out of their driveway. He lifts a hand, and I lift mine in return. We've got this social distancing thing down. Abbott follows my guidance to make a wide smooth semi-circle, and I drive him all the way back down the driveway where he does a square halt outside the barn doors. I walk forward to his head, and after he shoves his nose into my hand, I remove the lines and give his neck a pat.

Quit while you're ahead. It's something horses have taught me. There's a moment when they're giving you the best they can on that particular day, and if you reward them at that moment, you can start up the next day and keep learning without missing a beat.

Miss that elusive moment, and you could spend another hour trying to get back to where you were, and still not make it. The horse gets tired, you get tired, and the next session requires a lot of review.

Abbott knows he's done, and he knows what comes next. Every muscle is tensed, and little twitches run under his skin. I lift my hand in front of his face and he snorts but holds his ground.

He waits. I wait. *Four-three-two-one ...* I reach out and tap his shoulder and that's it. He jumps sideways, ducking his head low and letting out a much longer, louder snort.

After a few seconds he edges back, stepping to within a couple of feet of me then reaching his head and nose out to nudge my shoulder.

I laugh. "Abbott! You got me!"

It's not quite tag, but it's as close as I'd want to get with a thousand-pound animal.

It's definitely fun, and it reminds me of the bond I have with this horse, and in a weird way it tempts me to just turn him out in the field and stop working with him.

Because with my aunt's careful breeding, and Abbott's quick mind and aptitude for learning, every hour of work I put into him makes him worth more money, and I really don't ever want to be in a position where this horse is worth the exact amount of money I need to pay the taxes on the farm.

Boom. Back to reality where there's a pandemic and nobody's making any money.

"Oh, well. At least I was happy for a little while." I snap my fingers and Abbott follows me into the barn so I can untack him and send him out to the paddock with his buddies.

***

There's a message from Dan Summer. Thank you for your message Ms. Reilly. I can understand why you'd be uncertain, but I did mean to book for today. I'm returning to Ontario via New York and I need a place to spend my mandatory fourteen days of self-isolation. Because I may be more of a burden than a normal guest, as I will have to rely on you for my groceries and other essentials, I'm prepared to pay a twenty-five per cent premium on top of your usual rates. Please advise if this is satisfactory as I'll be arriving this evening and need somewhere to stay (I may arrive quite late).

No. Nuh-uh. He's coming from New York? What if he has the virus? What if he gets horrifically sick while he's staying in my loft?

But ... Not just the usual rates for fourteen days, but twenty-five per cent more. That completely makes up for having to cancel the week-long bookings of my two March Break families.

But, still no. It's weird. I get that he'll be in self-isolation, but I'll know he's there. And since there's nowhere for me to go, I'll always be here, and it will be strange.

But ... Where else is he going to go? The news may be full of terrible stories, but it's also full of stories of people doing good. How would I feel if I was caught away from home when a pandemic hit? This person is asking me to do one, small thing. To offer him shelter in a space that would otherwise be empty. And he's offering to pay me for it. Can I really say no?

I can't.

I hit reply and for the tiniest, most fleeting of moments it registers as odd that he called me Ms. Reilly because I thought I had it set up that my first name was all potential guests saw when they booked. I shake my head. I must be wrong. I'll have to login to my account later and double-check.

I type **Dear Mr. Summer, Of course, under the circumstances I'd be happy to welcome you here. Along with making up the bed, and providing fresh towels, I'll** put some basic provisions in the loft for now, and can fully stock it up the next time I go to the grocery store. The lock code for the door is 1-3-6-9 — please let yourself in whenever you arrive. I look forward to meeting you — from a distance! — tomorrow morning.

***

There's a shaft of sunlight falling across the wide-planked floor in the loft and I move my feet into it and enjoy the warmth that seeps through my cotton socks. From here the view is expansive. The house and barn are already built on a slight rise in the land, and the land itself is several meters up from the river. As always, when I look out the loft windows, I can hear The Who's hit, "I Can See for Miles" in my head.

I used to live here. Before my aunt got really sick – when she just needed me nearby to take care of the horses and the property, and to check in regularly – I slept in the loft; never closing the curtains, letting the morning light wake me naturally and watching the star-sprayed skies as I fell asleep.

Before that, when it was neglected and dusty – full of boxes and the only furniture was disassembled – Dob and I used to come up here. Back then the view I would marvel at was his collarbone, or the ripple of his ribs ... until he'd get so close that I couldn't see those things anymore. Until his body was pressed so tightly against mine it became all about feeling, instead of looking.

There's a squeal outside – it sounds like Lemon – which snaps me back to attention. She needs a good, long conditioning outing to take some of the edge off her.

I look around the space. Coffee maker on the counter, where Mr. Summer will see it right away ... *check*. Fluffy towels visible on the towel rack in the ensuite at the far end of loft ... *check*. Homemade quilt smoothed tight over a soft blanket and flannel sheets designed to keep out the chill of the still-cool evenings ... *check*.

I step out to the small landing in front of the door, pull it closed tight behind me, press the keypad to lock it and call out, "Hey, Ms. Lemon. Stop causing trouble. You're coming with me!"

***

I settle lightly into Lemon's saddle and a quick tension jolts through her. Like a shiver – in at her neck and out around her tail. As long as I let it pass through she's fine, but I know, without a doubt, that were I to grip with my legs, or take the reins up too quickly, or even to tense inwardly, she'd be accelerating in a hot second.

I look up the driveway and that's all it takes. This horse doesn't need aids in the way most horses do. Whatever subtle shifts happen in my body when I move my eyes and think about going forward, tell her all she needs to know. She flares her nostrils, and points her ears, and swings into a long-striding walk.

At the top of the driveway she's full of questions, transmitted to me via our private channel. *Which direction?* she wants to know, along with, *Can we go faster?*

Left. Walk.

She turns left. *I'd rather trot.*

Not now.

Halfway to Charlie and Bree's driveway, she checks in ... *Just wondering ...?*

Still no.

I know she wants to go. I get it. But there's still snow in shady places. The daytime highs aren't hitting double digits yet – or rarely – and it's common to walk through pockets of very-cool-air-indeed in places where the road dips. In other words, this isn't pre-season training; it's pre-pre-a-season-that's-definitely-going-to-be-delayed.

There's lots of time to go faster ... and just me thinking it raises a little jig-jog from her. *Oh, Lemon ... no, sweetheart.*

Because she's energetic, and gets year-round turnout, the mare's baseline fitness level is relatively very good, but not good enough to let her trot any distance on the gravel roads with my weight on her back during the first week of our training schedule.

Agatha pays me to bring her mares on slowly. I take pride in handing them to her beautifully conditioned and absolutely sound.

We'll walk.

Of course, keeping up a forward, active walk over several kilometres is harder than Lemon believes it's going to be. Eventually her requests to break into a trot space out. Eventually we both relax and enjoy the sun and the breeze.

We've put about six kilometres behind us, and Lemon's settled into a steady rhythm. When I run my hand along her neck it's slightly damp, and I'm thinking ahead to dismounting at the end of the driveway, and lifting her saddle off so she can cool down and dry out as we walk to the barn, when she floods with tension again, and her ears sweep forward, and her neck bows into a high arch, and she dances underneath me.

"What is it?" I exhale, and spread my toes in my boots – my own personal tricks to dispel my body's tension – and I scratch her withers, and she quietens slightly, but she's still not sure.

She sends out a rattling snort. *There's a scary thing there.*

"What scary thing?"

A thing that doesn't belong.

"Whatever it is, it's made of metal, Lemon. Metal can't move on its own."

Things that can move on their own can hide behind metal. They can hide behind the metal, and wait for me, then jump – aarrgghh!! Somebody said jump!

She leaps sideways beneath me – her body fluid as a snake – and I let my hips follow her, keep my leg pressure on at a reassuring level, and don't – for the love of god, absolutely do not – grab the reins.

I need to save myself. And you, too, I guess.

"I know, honey. And you're doing a good job. But I need you to stand still for one minute while I look at the scary thing."

It's a pile of buckets, and there's a hand-lettered sign leaning against them, and I memorize the phone number on it as quickly as I can because the pile actually does look quite precarious, and the sign is at a not-completely-stable angle, and the wind is gusting every now and then, and if those buckets tumble down, all the Zen, horse-whispering calmness in the world isn't going to keep me from being whisked off at high-speed for a hammering gallop down the road.

* * *

Walk?

Bree's text comes in as I'm watching Lemon drop to her knees and roll back and forth; grinding her freshly groomed coat in the mud.

I'll come over now. I want to talk to Cleo anyway.

Cleo's cleaning the chicken coop. "You want some eggs?" She gestures to a basket with half-a-dozen eggs lying on a nest of straw.

"Hmm ... actually ... maybe I do. If Bree doesn't want them. Here she comes; she can let me know."

"Let you know what? If I can spare you any toilet paper?" She tips her sunglasses down and winks, and I'm rushed with affection for her silly sense of humour, and her natural style that means even out here, standing in a yet-to-bloom bleak spring landscape, quarantined from the world, she pulls together an outfit of Canadian Tire rubber boots, and a set of sunglasses from the army surplus store, with a scarf knitted by Charlie's mother, to look like a fashion influencer, if fashion influencers also had the organizational skills to keep the spring planting moving forward by cooking and delivering a hot four-course lunch for six to the middle of a farm field.

"Gosh, now that you mention it, I might need that, as well as the eggs."

Cleo shifts to stand in front of the chicken coop door as a hen makes a run for it. "What's up?"

"I have a booking for the loft."

"You had a booking for the loft, and you canceled it." Bree says.

"I know, but after I canceled it, it didn't even occur to me to block the date off, because – I mean, who's traveling right now? – and some guy booked it for fourteen days because he's coming back from the states and he needs somewhere to self-isolate ... and, he wants to pay me twenty-five per cent more, because I need to provide food for him."

"Hence the eggs," Cleo says.

"Yeah, if you guys don't need them, I can get brownie points by putting a couple in the loft for him – city types always love the 'freshly laid' egg thing." I turn to Bree. "I was kidding about the toilet paper, though. I keep a separate supply for the rental properties."

A swirl of wind gusts across the yard and Bree adjusts her scarf. "I need to walk, and while we walk I'll consider whether I approve of your pandemic vacation booking."

"First ..." I point at Cleo. "I have a thought for you."

"A thought about what?"

"About 4H. Do you think maple syrup is an acceptable agricultural fund-raising activity?"

Her eyes widen. "What? Where? How?"

I point to the woodlot. "Last I checked there were maples in there. Which, between me and your family, we already own. And earlier today Lemon and I stumbled across a bunch of used sap buckets for sale. So, I wondered ..."

"Oh. My. Wow. I need to go inside and do some research ..." She takes two steps toward the house, turns back, latches the coop door, then starts jogging, calling over her shoulder. "I'll email you later Aspen!"

Bree and I walk through the woods. Sound, wind, and light are all dampened as soon as we step between the trees. Limbs meet overhead, and roots criss-cross the foot-worn paths. The woodlot's compact enough that at the very edge of our vision is a glow of the daylight outside, and way, way up at the highest point of the canopy, branches sway in the wind. It intensifies the feeling that this is a small bubble of peace. It's also the same as it's ever been, and for a few moments it's easy to forget the whole world is different.

In here, it isn't.

"It's really nice of you to suggest the maple syrup thing to Cleo," Bree says.

I point to a wide trunk with pieces of wood nailed at even intervals along the bark. "It's a surprise nobody's done it before." Further along this path a rope dangles from a tree where, for what seemed like years, a deer head dangled – part of an experiment Charlie's uncle was conducting to see how quickly insects would clear it to the bone. The answer was, not quickly. From our current vantage point, I can spot two of the half-dozen cross-country obstacles I've built over the years to make sure

Agatha's horses will jump anything that confronts them – even along a narrow path, even in the strange light of the woods. "Literally every other activity I can imagine has taken place in these woods."

"Hmm ... really? That's something I've never done in here."

"Oh, god, Bree ... that's not what I meant." I'm blushing, though, because I have a quick flash of bark against my back, Dob pressed up along my front. Of me reaching my hands overhead to grab a low branch, with my shirt lifting high in the process. Of Dob's hands skimming up along my bare skin, cupping my breasts so I giggled, even as I found my grip on the branch and used the leverage to lift my legs, circle his waist with them, and squeeze him tight.

We'd been at a bonfire at Charlie and Bree's. I said I was going to the bathroom, Dob said he was going for another beer, and we'd left, together, hand-in-hand.

That's how we did everything for a while. Hand-in-hand. Side-by-side. Having each other's backs.

Then there was the wedding, where Dob said he was going for a beer ... and I haven't seen him since, and now nobody's allowed to walk hand-in-hand.

Bree and I step out of the woodlot and into the field, still brownish-grey with last year's winter-killed grasses.

We skirt the edge of the trees, and a shard of sun makes it through the thin cloud covering, and Bree pauses, and turns her face to the sky. "That sun is heavenly! I heard some really good advice earlier today that said it's definitely a bad idea to think about things right now. Instead of thinking, you should just *be*."

"Bree, you have to stop watching the Style and Wellness network. Which 'doctor' said that?" I lift my hands in the air to put quotes around "doctor."

"Aspen, that's mean. Most of them are actual, legit doctors."

"Bree, I had a Doctor of Wood Sciences stay in the loft for a long weekend last year. I definitely wouldn't take pandemic advice from him."

"Maybe you should. It sounds very soothing to study wood for your Ph.D."

We stop in front of a low-slung cabin tucked up against the woodlot. Snugged up against the trees, the view from the back windows is green and woodsy – guests can watch squirrels jump from branch to branch while they wash their dishes – whereas the big front windows look out on the river, which is so close Bree and I can hear the gulls squawking as we climb up on the porch.

I spread my palm against the weathered wood siding. "Maybe you're right. The silver of this cedar does calm me. Or maybe that's this whole place."

Bree leans against the railing and makes a frame with her fingers and thumbs. "This is an amazing spot. Have you ever thought of moving down here from the farmhouse?"

The ache hits me. The one that blooms right under my breastbone whenever I think about something I really, really want, but doubt I'll ever get. Often it's about Dob, but sometimes the idea of making my own perfect home in this perfect spot gets me, too. It's silly, though. I'm already incredibly lucky, and I live about three-hundred metres away from this dream spot, and I can come here every day if I want ... as long as I can keep paying the taxes. As long as I don't lose the farm. *Get over it.* I shrug to show Bree I'm fine, no big deal. "In my wildest dreams, yes. You know – the dreams where money isn't an object, and I can afford to move out of a perfectly good house and do the major renovations it would take to convert this from a cute vacation cabin to a year-round home."

Bree winks. "So not till next year, then?"

To be fair, at this time last year the cabin was unusable, and now it's more-or-less three-season habitable, and I wouldn't have guessed that was possible.

It was John who made it happen. I first met him at Easter last year, when he was one of two guys who booked into my loft to attend a friend's wedding on the island. He called again, in July, reminding me who he was, saying he'd been given a few days off unexpectedly and would love to come back if the loft wasn't already booked. Which, all through July and August, it was.

"In that case, I don't suppose there's any chance you'd rent me that cabin on your property? The one near the woods. I noticed it when I was there at Easter. It has a great view."

"I couldn't rent you that," I'd said. "It was last used as a hunting cabin, and that was twenty years ago. It's definitely on the dilapidated side of rustic."

He'd been quiet for a second before saying, "Listen, this might be completely inappropriate for me to even suggest, and if you think it is, go ahead and tell me no, but I fell in love with your island, and I really love working with my hands, and I might go crazy if I don't get out of the city for at least a few days, so if you'd let me bring my camping gear, and stay in that cabin, I could do some work on it and maybe you could rent it to other people in the future."

"Would you be bringing your partner?" I'd asked.

"My partner?"

"Um, what was his name? Will?"

"Oh," he'd said. And there was something in that "oh" that told me everything. How wrong I'd gotten it, and that the really good-looking, polite, and friendly guy who I'd assumed was gay, wasn't. And that he probably did like the island and need a break, but that he also wanted to see me again. And in a rare moment of bravery, and hope, and self-indulgence, I'd pushed thoughts of Dob out of my head and said, "Why not?"

He stayed a week and he slept in my bed the whole time, and we worked on the cabin most days, and he was good with his hands – in every sense – and when he left the cabin was weathertight and on the charming side of rustic.

Truth be told, it's not the siding that's making me smile. It's the memory of John and me stepping out here for a late-afternoon break which ended with me on my back with the sun-warmed planks underneath me. The weight of his body pressing me against the hard boards made me breathless, and when I kissed his shoulder it was salty. The memory sends a tiny shiver of remembered pleasure through me.

"I know," Bree says. "It *is* cold. Let's go in."

I punch the code into the new lock pad on the ancient door, and there's no heat inside, but thanks to John's insulation, and the absence of the wind gusting off the St. Lawrence, it's relatively comfortable.

Bree walks around, her sock feet silent on the old barn board floors. She pauses by the big window and turns to me. "This place has so much potential."

I nod. "All credit to John. It wouldn't be inhabitable without him."

"Well ... yes ... it is inhabitable, and clearly John's a decent handyman, but it could be much better."

Bree's got a flash in her eyes I've seen a few times. When she asked if I'd like to try canning tomatoes and I said, "Sure," meaning someday, and with some planning, and the next thing I knew she'd bought three bushels and I got a phone call saying, "You have to bring any mason jars you own, and come over here to help me, STAT!"

Or when she decided to make customized fortune cookies for the guests at her wedding and we sat up until 2:30 a.m. with tweezers, and scissors, and tiny scraps of paper removing the standard fortunes, and inserting ones she'd printed off herself.

I love her but I'm not sure the middle of a pandemic is the right time to let Bree's creative side loose. "What do you mean?"

"Well, since you ask, while watching the Style and Wellness network you're so fond of dissing, I saw a really interesting segment on re-decorating with what you already have around – since we can't exactly shop – and I have a basement full of paint, and fabric, and even some furniture, that would work for a lot of the ideas they suggested."

"Really? What kind of ideas?"

"Why do you sound worried, Aspen?"

"I can't think why ... oh wait ... your floor refinishing project."

Bree puts her hands on her hips. "You only know about that because you're my oldest friend, and that's the exact same reason you should have the decency not to bring it up. Besides, the guy at the rental depot never told me you have to start the machine with the sandpaper *off* the floor ..." She shrugs. "Whatever. If you don't want to charge a couple of hundred dollars more a week for this place, I won't help you."

"You figure? That much?"

"At least," Bree says. "Come here."

I close the distance between us, wondering if I should, wondering how close Bree really wants me to get.

I have my answer as she reaches out and hooks my shoulders, then turns us both around to gaze out the window where the sky is starting to show the first wisps of a classic orange-and-pink island sunset.

"Leave it with me."

Four

Consciousness seeps in the same way the daylight does. Slowly, gently, incrementally. Its leisurely arrival allows me to note how heavy my limbs are. My head's fuzzy. I lift my hand to feel creases in my cheek. I can't remember the last time I slept so deeply.

My awakening might be gradual, but it's also inexorable. The sun's not going down until it's completed its day's circuit and I'm not sleeping again until I've cleaned, fed, and exercised four horses, and myself, and ... *oh yeah* ...

I sit up so swiftly I have to pause, perched on the edge of the mattress, to wait out the sudden blood pressure drop.

Sure enough, when I rise and pull the curtains back there's a small, unfamiliar car parked on the far side of my truck.

My guest is here.

Although it's unsettling that I didn't wake up – even partially – when he arrived. I'm just as glad I didn't. I wouldn't have gone properly back to sleep, and the kind of full-on, drugged-like eight hours I had last night is a gift.

Downstairs, with the kettle building to a full boil, and the radio telling me the Olympics have been canceled – the *Olympics* – I'm torn. The host in me feels I should be hustling out to greet my new guest, introduce myself, make sure he has what he needs.

But ... he's here because he's in self-isolation so I have to keep my distance. I won't even be stepping into the loft until after he's gone; I'll have to put clean sheets on the doorstep for him and he can change his own bed. The chimes that precede the hourly news on the radio remind me that what's sleeping in to me is still very early, for most people and given how late Mr. Summers arrived, he's probably still asleep.

I pour my tea, boot up my laptop, and figure there's plenty of time when I'm out working in the barn for us to say a nicely distanced hello.

I check my email to see John's sent out a group message, forwarding information from the government press office about emergency support programs announced by the government.

There's a round-up newsletter from the CBC – Your morning news headlines – um, yeah, the world as we know it is upside-down. Done.

I skip right to the message from Cleo with the subject line, **Buckets!** It makes me smile, thinking of Jack Armstrong calling a Raptors game. Which would be great if the NBA hadn't been the first sports league to call a total shutdown. Everything these days is bittersweet.

Except Cleo. Hearing from her is just sweet.

There's not much to the message. It says **Yes! Let's do the maple syrup! I'll come by later today. P.S. I'm so excited!!!** There's a signature at the bottom of her email that says, **Oh Hello Day! Let's Do This.**

It makes me smile. It gets me out the door to the barn.

***

There's a dog asleep in the barn. Even though that's probably what should freak me out, the actual thing that freaks me out is that he's sleeping on the ancient, many-times-ripped-and-patched-up dog bed my aunt's ancient Border Collie, Tweed, slept on until the day he couldn't get up from it anymore and the vet made a house call to euthanize him.

I can imagine a dog using Tweed's dog flap to wander out of the overnight frost into the coziness of a barn warmed by four horses. I can't imagine it going into the tack room and digging out the bed that's been propped up against the wall for about four years now.

I stare at the dog and he lifts his head to return my gaze, thumping his tail twice, yawning, and lowering his head back to the bed. He's big, black-and-tan, and as far as I can tell I've never seen him before.

I turn to Campbell, watching me watch the dog and say, "Where did he come from?"

Campbell does this twitching thing with her eyes that makes it look like she's raising her eyebrows. "You don't know either, huh?"

I open the barn doors wide to let in the strengthening morning sun, move from stall to stall running my eyes and my hands over each horse. I look for anything out of place – blood, swelling. Nothing. They're all good.

The only thing out of place is the elephant – or the dog – in the room.

"Weird ..." I shake my head each time I walk by him. Everything about him is weird. My presence doesn't disturb him. That's weird. And since he's not afraid of me, I'm surprised he's not looking for food. Strange.

And the bed thing – I still have enough sleep woolliness in my head that I don't even want to try to figure that one out.

I walk down the aisle, opening each door, saying "Wait" at each stall. They all do, until I get to Campbell. She gets a, "Come on, then," and steps out into the aisle next to me. "OK!" I call over my shoulder, and the other three follow us out to the gate, which I push wide and hold as they file through.

Some mornings they stop dead, heads down, the minute they enter the field. Other times, they roll, and roll. Occasionally, when the temperature, or the atmospheric pressure, or something is just right, they explode, bucking and running.

Today they seem to be starting their day the way I did. Slow, easy, languid. They drift into the frost-tipped field. They stroll around, noses down, looking for patches of grass that have already been hit by the morning sun thawing them from crisp and white, to breakfast material. The horses are all as relaxed as the strange dog in my barn, and I guess that's a good sign – at least his presence didn't freak them out.

Campbell pauses, lifts her nose, and whickers, and I say, "Have fun. I'll be back when it's time for you guys to work."

I pull the gate closed, double-loop the chain, and strike out for the barn already mentally wheeling the barrow into place outside Campbell's stall.

"Aspen?"

Now I know what it means when your heart jumps to your throat. It means your throat has trouble swallowing, and your lungs have trouble breathing, and your heart has trouble beating, and your whole body starts tingling from lack of oxygen, or blood, or plain-and-complete-shock that the person you're supposed to be over, but still think about at least once every day, is standing on the stairs leading to the loft over your barn.

Or at least that's what it means to me as I stand and stare at Dob.

***

There was a time when I would have run to him. There was a time when I might have screamed at him and bent down to pick up the rock by my feet and hurl it at him.

Maybe I've mellowed, or maybe it's social distancing, or maybe after he broke my heart it made me a little dead inside, because all I do is make a choking noise and retreat to the barn.

The dog's still there. On the bed that isn't his. What the absolutely-crazy-incomprehensible-hell, is going on?

Even as I lift the pitchfork from its hook, part of my brain is watching my hand do it, thinking *well, this is a strange way to react,* even while another part of my brain is stating the only single thing I know for sure right now, which is that these stalls have to get done.

I'm standing in Campbell's door when my phone rings. Bree.

"Hi."

"You sound weird."

"I am weird. My life is weird."

"In what way?"

A body breaks the stream of daylight brightening the barn. "My mystery guest? Self-isolation man? It's Dob."

"Dob!" I don't even have to glance in his direction to be sure he's heard her shriek.

I nod. "Dob." To me, my voice sounds flat. I wonder if it sounds flat to him.

"But you didn't say it was Dob ..."

"Because he didn't say it was him! He booked under Dan Summer."

"Oh. Why didn't you tell me that? I might have figured it out ... Dobson Daniel Summerton ..."

Shit. So those are two things I feel – ambushed and stupid. I sneak a sideways glance at Dob's feet – oh my god, they're bare – and I feel a pinprick of annoyance at him for making me feel stupid and ambushed, but there's no rush of full-on anger. I don't have time to wonder about it because Bree's still talking, "... but why didn't he use his own name?"

"He probably thought I wouldn't let him stay." For the first time I look straight at him. I narrow my eyes to telegraph that I certainly would *not* have let him stay.

"OK, I have a very big question."

"Yes?" I'm waiting for her to ask if I *am* going to let him stay and how quickly I'm going to kick him out.

"Does he still look good?"

"God, Bree! No!" It does make me look at him again, though. I mean, yeah, he's gorgeous, but he's got this self-satisfied smile tugging at the corners of his mouth. Did he used to smile like that? Did I used to find it hot?

"No, he doesn't?" she prompts.

"No, you can't ask that."

"So, he does."

"He's standing right here. He's listening to our conversation."

"What's he doing?"

I lean forward, narrow my eyes more. "He's smirking."

That gets a reaction. He jerks back, and furrows his brow. "I'm not smirking."

"La, la, la ..."

"What are you doing?" Bree asks.

"He's trying to talk to me. He's trying to say he's not smirking, but I'm not listening."

"Wow, this got immature fast," Dob says.

"Hey Bree, the guy who snuck into my loft at night, and used a fake name, just called me immature."

"It's not a fake name," he says.

"It's not exactly a fake name," Bree says.

"Et tu, Bree?"

"No," she says. "Sorry. He's wrong. You're right. Where has he been? Where did he come from?"

I sigh. Tuck the phone between my shoulder and cheek as I pick up the pitchfork. "As if I know. He said New York, but his car has Ontario plates, and honesty is not exactly his first policy."

From over my shoulder I hear, "I've been in Yukon. I bought the car from a guy there – he was from Kenora – I drove home through New York; caught the US ferry."

I turf a pile of manure toward the wheelbarrow, without looking. If Dob's standing too close, that should back him off. "Did you year that? He says he drove from Yukon via New York."

"Well, that was stupid."

I dump a wet patch of shavings into the barrow. "You want stupid, he's in bare feet."

"In the barn?"

"In the doorway. In March. When it was – what? – minus two overnight?"

"Well, I guess it's warmer than Yukon."

"If he really was in Yukon."

Dob's bare feet make no sound on the gravel outside, but I know he's gone because in his absence the morning sun floods uninterrupted into the barn. His rapid departure doesn't upset me either. I pinch my arm to make sure I'm not completely numb. "Ow!"

"Are you OK? What happened?"

"Never mind. It's nothing."

Bree's sigh fills my ear. "What on earth are you going to do?"

"I'll let you know when I convince myself this is actually happening." While I'm talking something wet nudges into my palm. I look down to see the dog, big liquid eyes fixed on me, tail swaying. "At least I figured one thing out. I think I know where this dog came from, and how he got old Jessie's bed."

"Dog? What dog?"

I sigh. "Let's catch up later. We have a lot to talk about. In the meantime it's not like Dob is going to do my chores for me."

***

I dump the wheelbarrow three times while cleaning the stalls. Each time I do my best not to look up at the loft windows.

Each time the dog comes with me.

In the interests of not spending my morning not-staring at the loft, I pull on my running gear and run 10K at my quickest 5K pace.

As I come back along the driveway I look at the loft, but only in a sweeping view across the whole property. Far line of evergreens? *Check.* River? *Still there.* Paddock with three of four grazing horses visible? *Yup.* Barn, with loft on top of it? *Appears to be intact.* I keep scanning across to the woodlot, and that makes me think of Cleo, who

Bree told me would be by this afternoon, and I decide to get a move-on working with Abbott.

I pull him out of the field and, for the first time, add a breast collar and neck band, with traces attached, to the surcingle girth I've been using during his long-lining sessions.

He doesn't bat an eyelash at the new equipment and walks in the same, rock-solid manner, he did in our last session. When I lean back on the traces, he hesitates and stops, but as soon as I tell him to walk on, I can feel him lean in, and as he pulls me forward I have nothing else on my mind except the pleasure of showing this young horse what he can do, and the reward of having him figure it out so easily.

When I ask him to "whoa" he stops smoothly, and I give him a big scratch on his withers and ask, "How about trying one more thing?"

For the next step I pick up the half-red-painted, half-scuffed-to-bare-metal single tree that's been around here longer than I have. Every year I watched my aunt use it to train horses to pull. Now, for the first time, I'm the one using it.

I show it to Abbott who cocks his ears slightly forward. Then I drop it to the ground in front of him. No flinching. No nothing. I walk all around him, jiggling it to make the clips jingle, dropping it repeatedly. His ears follow me, but I've trained him to stand while I do all sorts of strange things around him and his deep sigh, and slow shifting of weight from one leg to the other seems to say, *"Listen, if I could handle the bubble wrap, I can handle this."*

OK, then. Time for him to pull it.

I secure each trace to one end of the tree – slip knotting them with binder twine in case I need to free him quickly, then I take up my usual long-lining position, ask him to walk forward ...

... and he does.

Willingly, easily, and smoothly.

The weight of the tree is less than the weight I applied when I leaned back on the traces, but the tree is jerkier, and makes a fair bit of noise – especially when I steer Abbott out of the ring and onto the gravel driveway.

He doesn't seem to care, though. He pulls the pinging, clinking piece of metal up and down the driveway. He makes a nice, rounded turn at each end, when I ask him to, and I decide to follow my own advice and quit right now, while I'm much further ahead than I could ever have dreamed I'd be.

***

I've had a shower and I'm finishing my lunch, when Cleo cracks the kitchen door open. "Hello?"

"Hey, you. Just in time for a chocolate chip cookie." I gesture to the tin sitting on the counter next to the door.

She reaches over, pulls out a cookie, then steps back to the doorstep.

It's not like we're always hugging each other under normal circumstances, but her care to hover just outside, and my awareness of not stepping too close to her are evident. I might have time for a pang of sadness if she didn't wink, and say, "I hear home-baking will be like gold soon."

"Oh yeah? Why's that?"

"Haven't you heard? Flour's the new toilet paper."

"Is that so?"

She nods. "This pandemic is going to make us all desperate for things we never knew we wanted."

I glance past her at the loft. "Well, I have toilet paper and flour, so hopefully that means I'm safe."

"By the way," she says. "What's with the dog?" She steps back and, sure enough, Dob's dog is sitting at the edge of the driveway.

"It's a long story. Let's get the horses tacked up and I'll tell you later."

Forty-five minutes later, Cleo and I are turning Campbell and Mocha into the sap bucket driveway. The buckets are still there, although the sign's blown over. Rock steady Campbell doesn't even look at them, and since Campbell's not worried, Mocha marches right by them as well.

Dob's dog – who seems to have become my dog – trots alongside.

As we near the house two very-much-smaller dogs come flying off the porch, ears and hackles up. They bark, and bark, and bark some more, and Dob's big black-and-tan dog quietly shuffles his rangy body underneath Mocha and lies down there.

"I'm going to call him Pearson," I tell Cleo.

She knits her eyebrows then relaxes them. "Ah ... because of the Peace prize."

A bent-backed man appears from a large, once-red, now largely peeled-to-grey-wood shed and his little dogs fall back to let him take over. "We don't want no trespassers around here!"

Pearson whines, while Cleo clucks Campbell forward a step. "Well, then, you shouldn't put things you're trying to sell at the end of your driveway."

"There's a phone number there. I thought all you kids lived on your phones these days."

"Well obviously you don't, or you'd know your phone's out of service. I tried to call you four times." Cleo shrugs. "Do you want to sell the sap buckets, or not?"

He grunts. "Well, since you're here now. I got thirty of 'em. I want ten bucks each. No negotiating. Take it or leave it."

Cleo asks Campbell for a lovely turn on the forehand, then clucks the mare back toward the drive. She snaps her fingers. "C'mon Pearson," and she doesn't have to say anything to me. With the boss mare on the move, Mocha's already heading off after her.

"Hey now!" the old man calls.

Cleo stops Campbell, and looks over her shoulder. "Yes?"

"Where're you going?"

"You said take it or leave it, so I'm leaving. I'm fourteen years old and I'm trying to raise money for a 4H trip – what do you think I am? Made of money?"

"Hmph," he says. "Well, then make me an offer."

We turn the horses back to face him, and Cleo scans the property, letting her gaze linger on the shed. "Looks like you need some painting done around here."

"What of it?"

"You need painting and I need sap buckets." She waits. Doesn't speak. The man shifts his weight from one foot to the other. I'm starting to think Cleo should become a lawyer – or something involving negotiation.

I'm ready to turn Mocha around again, when the man says, "You supply the paint."

"I can do that."

"But it has to be good paint. None of that watery shit."

"I'm not using oil."

"Your choice, kid. If it peels off, you're coming back."

Cleo drops her voice, mutters, "It'll probably last longer than you."

"Cleo!" I say.

"What's that, kid?" the man says.

Cleo cups her hands around her mouth. "It'll last as long as you need it to."

The man's taken a couple of steps toward us. He blinks. All the testiness is gone from his voice, replaced by softness, "Are you Nancy Shields' granddaughter?"

If I didn't know Cleo – and Campbell – so well, and if I hadn't watched Cleo's shoulders shaking all through her grandmother's funeral not quite a year ago, I probably wouldn't notice her slight flinch, which in turn causes Campbell to prick her ears and lift her head. The sauciness is gone from Cleo's voice, too, when she says, "Yes."

He nods. "You probably don't know this, but your grandmother brought me a hot cooked dinner every Sunday after my wife died."

Cleo blinks. "She was a good cook."

"You can say that again. It was the only day of the week I didn't have a peanut-butter sandwich for dinner."

My throat's thick. I want to hug Cleo, and hug the old man who misses her grandmother, and, of course, I can't hug anyone right now. When Cleo says, "Thank you for telling me," Campbell turns her head around and bumps Cleo's foot; there's nothing like a horse for giving a person what they need.

Cleo's words from earlier flash through my mind – how we're all going to be desperate for things we didn't know we wanted – she might not have known she wanted a new and lovely memory of her grandmother, but now she has it, it's something she can hang onto forever.

"So, we have a deal, young lady?" I smile to notice Cleo's gone from "kid" to "young lady."

Cleo nods. "We'll pick the buckets up before they all blow over at the end of your driveway. I'll do the painting in a couple of weeks – as soon as the temperature stays warm enough to let the paint cure."

Cleo and I ride down the driveway and I want to say something deep and meaningful about her grandmother, but it's not like I have anything to say she doesn't already know.

She turns to me, with a big smile spread across her face, and says, "Well, that's awesome, because I have a thousand dollars in my savings account from selling my 4H calf last year and now I don't have to spend any of it on the buckets."

I let out a short, sharp, laugh, and she says, "What?"

I shake my head. "Nothing. You're going to be OK."

"Of course I am. I have plans. Maybe we can use some of the money to build a sap house. Maybe next year we'll tap twice as many trees ..."

I decide anytime the news starts getting me down, I'll listen to Cleo spinning her ideas instead.

Five

The rain starts with a smattering of drops as Cleo and I get back from our ride.

I pull the horses in early, throw them some hay and find myself grateful for the intensity and steadiness of the downpour that lasts throughout the afternoon and until well after the light dies from the sky. It means there's no reason for me to be out and around the barn. No reason for Dob to be there, either.

No reason for us to cross paths.

Although, I do have his dog. "He's good at abandoning people, isn't he?" I ask Pearson, who's stretched out under my kitchen table in the warm spot where the vent blows hot air in.

Pearson lets his tail lift and fall, and I Google What to feed a dog if you have no dog food.

Good thing I'm going grocery shopping tomorrow.

Which does pose a dilemma, in that for a twenty-five per cent extra fee, I agreed to feed Dob. When I didn't know he was Dob. Which, possibly, renders our agreement moot. Still, common decency and all that ...

Shopping for Pearson is one thing. He'll get whatever dog food they have in the grocery store aisle, and if it's one of those big brands modern dog owners love to decry – oh well – I'm sure Pearson will like it and it will keep him from starving.

But Dob. Obviously I could just buy him bread, and milk, and apples, and a few boxes of Kraft Dinner, but I'm sure there are a few particular items he'd like. I know the prospect of spending the next I'm-not-sure-how-long mostly on my own property, is made much more bearable by the promise of settling down every evening with a mug of salted caramel hot chocolate, and a Nanaimo bar.

I had visions of how this would work. Of my pandemic guest and me maintaining a healthy-but-friendly business relationship. Of me knocking on his door, then stepping down to the lower landing, and saying, "How are you today?" and "Is there anything I can do to make your stay more pleasant?"

Considering I still haven't spoken directly to Dob, that's not going to happen.

I look over to see Pearson, chin on paws, staring at me.

"Yeah, yeah, OK. You're right. I'm a professional."

I open my email, insert dds@email.com into the "To" field – and, yes, now that I know, it clearly stands for Dobson Daniel Summerton – and type. **Good evening. I** will be going to the grocery store tomorrow morning. Is there anything in particular you'd like me to pick up for you? Thank you.

It's as I'm nearly ready for bed, slotting my salted caramel hot chocolate mug into the dishwasher, that a response pings into my email. Thank you for asking. While there is already coffee here (thank you) I do drink a lot of it, so if you could buy some more, that would be great. If possible, half-and-half cream to go in it. And Double Stuf Oreos. Please. And thank you. Dob.

I reply. Understood.

Before I can shut down, there's another ping. Do you have my dog?

My fingers hover over the keyboard while replies spool through my head:

- *Oh, is that your dog?*

- *Dog? What dog?*

- *I see you haven't gotten any more careful with your relationships.*

But that would be engaging, and I'm not engaging.

Instead I take a picture of Pearson, back in his new favourite spot after a dinner of scrambled eggs served over pearl barley with some frozen peas and carrots mixed in. I send it to Dob, then shut down all my devices before he can reply.

***

I'm aware of the rain most of the night as a gentle tap-tapping on the tin roof. I listen to it, roll over, drift off, listen again, and repeat.

That is, until Pearson comes in and dedicates himself to licking my hand. I can't be angry, though. I have to be up early if I don't want to stand in line for an hour to get into the grocery store.

Everything outside is wet, but the horses are dry, and greet me with rustling of their bedding and deep-throated whickers.

I throw them out in the paddock and leave all the stall doors wide open, ready to be mucked when I get back.

Then I climb into the truck.

Think, I order myself. *Make sure you have everything.* I'm definitely not doing this for another week, at least. I've got to make sure this trip goes smoothly.

OK. *List.* I pat my pocket. *Yes.*

Shopping bins are on the seat beside me.

Gloves. Thankfully it's still chilly these mornings. I'll feel silly shopping in gloves in July if this stretches on that long. Or, maybe I won't. By then it might be completely normal.

Hand sanitizer. Yes. Dug out from under the sink in the bathroom where I'd never used it before.

I glance around before I turn the key in the ignition, and there's Dob. Out on the landing. Standing easily; feet hip-distance apart and still bare. Loose shorts, mussed hair, and no shirt.

It all comes rushing back to me – how he never seemed to have quite enough muscle to cover his bones. The ripple of his ribs under my hands.

It gives me the same pang as I got standing out there in the living room of my potential dream house with my perfect future captured in the view Bree was showing me.

Things I've wanted for a long time, but can't have.

Shit.

I shake my head. Missing the boat won't make me feel any better about the rest of this stuff. I fire the engine to life and gun the truck forward.

It feels odd, and somehow wrong, to be humming along the highway toward the ferry dock. A short trip I took for granted less than a week ago now seems like an expedition fraught with danger.

As I pull into an unusually short ferry line-up, and cut the engine, the absence of sound lets anxiety crowd in. The message on the electronic sign by the dock has been changed from **Obey all orders of crew members** to **Please stay in your vehicle while on the ferry.**

Don't worry. I have no desire to leave the confines of my own truck, containing only my own germs.

My friend Meg went through a period with her boyfriend, Jared, when he refused to leave the island. His dad had died and he was more or less fine as long as he stayed here, but the thought of going to the mainland filled him with angst.

I remember raising my eyebrows as she explained it to me.

I now totally, and completely understand.

But, I have two people and a dog to feed, and the grocery store is the same one I've gone to for years, and – sure – in some ways the whole world has changed, but in some ways it hasn't, and I need to do this.

The car in front of me rolls forward and I turn the key in the ignition, put the truck in gear, and ease forward after it.

It'll be fine. Everything will be just fine.

***

It's fine. I mean, it's weird. The store is so quiet. Everybody steers a wide berth around everybody else. If somebody's taking a good long look at pickles while you want olives, you have to stay back, patiently, and wait until they're done.

A large number of people are wearing masks, more are wearing gloves, and there are tape lines on the floor by the cashes showing how far back to wait from the shopper in front. Plexiglass shields have sprung up in front of the cashiers.

But there's enough of everything. There are even a few packs of toilet paper. I get two cans of coffee and two bags of double-stuffed Oreos. I grab a huge bag of dog food on sale.

The cashier is the one who often serves me. "How are you hun?" she asks as she scans my items, and the plexiglass hardly matters. "Big order for you," she says.

"I have a ... friend ... staying with me."

"That's nice." She nods. "It's not a good time to be alone."

"You take care, now sweetie," she calls as I leave, and I think of her standing there, serving dozens or hundreds of people in a shift, being cheerful through it all, and here I was afraid to get on the ferry.

Be braver, I admonish myself.

It's easy to be braver heading home, with a truck full of supplies, and no need to get back on the boat for another week or so.

I thumb a text to John. **How goes the battle?** Movement beyond my windshield makes me look up to see Charlie's cousin Ky, wearing his ministry-issued jacket and high-visibility vest waving to me.

I roll down my window, and from the requisite two metres away, Ky asks, "You been OK with all this?"

"I should be asking you. You're the essential service and all."

He shrugs. "Yeah. We know it when we sign up for the job. And it's not like we have to get really close to people – not like doctors." He shudders. "Couldn't pay me enough to do that job."

"Still," I say. "I appreciate what you're doing."

His eyes brighten. "You know who's doing something amazing?"

"From the look on your face I'm going to guess it's your wife." Ky and his wife Poppy are a well-known island love story. They've been inseparable since elementary school, and only got closer in the last couple of years as Poppy successfully fought breast cancer.

Ky grins. "You're right. She amazes me every day. But now she's set up this online noticeboard for the island, where people can ask for help, or give it. Here ..." He fishes in his pocket and pulls out a small card. "She printed up a bunch of these and told me to hand them out on the boat. The site's on there."

"It's a great idea, Ky. I'll definitely check it out as soon as I get a minute."

"Hmm ... yeah," he says. "I suppose you're busy. I hear Dob's back."

Whoa. Even though I should know better, the efficiency of the island rumour mill can still catch me off guard. "How'd you know that?"

"I work on the ferry, Aspen."

"I know, but he came in from the US."

"You still have to get on the boat after you cross the bridge. Like Dob did the night before everything shut down."

That's not what Dob told me. Still, deciding who to believe is a no-brainer. Deciding why Dob would say he took the other ferry is something a little harder to figure out.

I'm not about to get into that with Ky now. "Of course. You're right. For some reason I got it in my head that he was on the New York ferry, but it's way too early for that to be running."

Ky nods. "It never opens before Easter. Not sure when it'll start running with all this going on."

We've reached that point in the journey when the island is suddenly large, and real in front of us. Where islanders have learned to trust that no, we're not coming in too fast, and yes, the captain knows what he's doing, but tourists still sometimes get a little nervous.

Sure enough the throb of the engines drops to a hum, the big vessel settles into the water, and we traverse the final distance to the dock at a sedate glide.

Ky glances to the ramp, and gives me a salute, "Duty calls."

"Stay safe!" I call.

With few cars on the ferry, I'm rolling off in no time, waving at Ky standing beside the ramp, breathing a sigh of relief at being home when my tires hit the well-worn island highway.

***

In the kitchen I go through a multi-step unpacking process. Items for my fridge, items for my cupboards, and items to go into a separate box for Dob.

I carry the box up to the loft door and leave it there. No need to knock. The weather's still cool enough that the carton of milk won't spoil if it takes Dob a little while to bring it in.

It's just as well Dob and I aren't talking. I don't have time to chat. I need to tackle the barn.

I stop in the doorway. The barn is spotless.

All the stall doors are still open, but inside each one is only fluffy fresh bedding. And the floor doesn't bear a trace of anything – not a single speck of manure or scattered bedding.

Did Cleo come by ...? Pearson lifts his head from the old dog bed as though to remind me of the source of every single weird-and-unexpected thing in the last couple of days.

"Dob?" I ask him. He thumps his tail.

It could be, I guess ... goodness knows he watched me clean out this barn often enough when we were teenagers to know how it's done.

Back then I would have died to have him pitch in with me. Back when he was four-wheeler, and snowmobile, and motorbike-crazy, and I was horse-crazy.

In those days I was also Dob-crazy, but trying hard not to show it. He'd drop by when I was in the middle of barn chores – sometimes with Bree, who was his next-door neighbour, and sometimes alone – and I used to dream of him saying, "Let me give you a hand, then we can both go out for pizza, or ice cream," or ... anything. I didn't like motorcycles, but I would have ridden on the back of his, just for the chance to wrap my arms around his waist and spend time with him.

He never did, though. He'd always laugh as I pitched manure into the wheelbarrow and say, "Exactly why I like machines better than horses," then he'd head off.

So, if he's cleaned my barn today, I'll take it as a debt paid.

Which means I can get on with riding.

***

I put both Lemon and Mocha through some very early-season dressage work. It's all walking, using the quarter lines. A solid dose of leg-yielding – which I've never enjoyed, but which I have to fake enthusiasm for so I can ask the mares to do it. We also do turn-on-the-forehand, and turn-on-the haunches. Lemon's ace at turn-on-the-haunches since it involves continuously moving forward. Her overactive mind tends to get blown by turn-on-the-forehand, though. Fortunately, Mocha's quite good at that move so there's a bit of reward and a bit of pain in each ride.

Following the freeze-thaw, and snow, and wind of the winter, the sand ring footing is uneven and needs a good harrowing before I can use it for anything other than walking, so I take each mare for a trot up, then back down the driveway, before untacking and grooming them.

With that done, I glance at my phone. John's replied **Things are fine here. Lots of press releases to write! I'm very lucky to a) have an income, and b) not be doing dangerous work.** He's such a nice person. I look up at the loft. A truly, very nice person.

There's a text from Cleo, too. **My dad's picking the sap buckets up this aft. Can I get him to drop half off at your place for you to wash? Google says soap and hot water is fine. I'll wash the other half and we'll be good to go tomorrow a.m., if that works.**

I thumb back, **Yes and yes**, then my rumbling stomach tells me I need to have lunch.

After lunch I go to the shed containing all my aunt's driving gear. This is where I got the iron tree I used with Abbott the other day. The space in the middle of the shed is taken up by a flatbed wagon with a simple bench seat, and removable sides. It's easy to hitch, versatile, and great to teach young horses to pull reliably.

Various pieces of harness hang on hooks along the walls, and leaning up on the left-hand wall is a homemade arena drag I made with a wooden shipping pallet and railroad spikes. I keep a couple of cinderblocks stacked by the sand ring to throw on the drag and give it some weight. With Campbell's help I've used it to keep the footing in great shape over the last few years.

Today I carry it out of the shed, place it at the edge of the ring, and go to get Abbott from the paddock.

He's watched his mom do this work dozens, if not a hundred times, I've worked with him since he was a foal, and he's already pulled the tree with no problem, but still

... butterflies bat my stomach. I'm about to ask him to do something new and I don't know how he's going to react.

The thing about stepping outside your comfort zone, though, is there's only one way to do it.

I send Bree a text. **About to ask Abbott to pull the sand ring drag for the first time ever. If I don't text you back in an hour come by and see if I need an ambulance. Wish me luck! Xo**

We start by long-lining which, by now, is nothing for Abbott. Then I attach the traces to the tree and hook the drag onto that, and take one deep breath in, roll my shoulders back, give my hands a gentle shake, and say, "Walk on."

He takes a step forward, then another, then the drag bites into a clump of footing, and he stops. His ears flick back to me. This is a thing I've always liked about working with this horse. When he's not sure, he shows me he's not sure, then he waits for me to help him. "Walk on, Abbott," I say.

He does, and the drag moves along nicely until it hits another heavy area when I quickly say, "Walk on." This time Abbott gives me a hesitation instead of a halt, and I tell him he's a good boy.

We follow a Zamboni pattern I worked out with Campbell a long time ago; meaning Abbott never retraces his own steps, and never has to do a really tight turn. The first couple of turns take some adjustment from both of us, because the resistance of the drag is uneven as Abbott turns, and unlike when I'm just long-lining him, I have to avoid stepping on the drag, but we figure it out.

I didn't add the cinderblocks this time, so the harrowing wasn't as deep as it could have been, but the ring looks beautifully inviting. I walk up beside Abbott, and rub his neck and say, "Next time we'll add the weight and it will be even better," and he noses me, and as he's doing that, Charlie and Bree's truck rolls up the driveway and Charlie gets out.

I call over, "For a minute there I thought it was Bree coming to make sure I hadn't killed myself driving Abbott."

"Nope. Just me bringing you sap buckets. Where do you want them?"

"Might as well put 'em there by the walkway to the house. I guess I'll be washing them in the kitchen."

I unhitch Abbott while Charlie unloads the buckets and we meet on the gravel, two metres apart. "So, this is what it's come to ..." Charlie waves at the space between us.

I grin. "Yeah, well, I'm no longer pure. I went to Food Basics this morning."

Charlie grins back. "I never thought Ms. Pregent's old 'Sex Degrees of Separation' lecture would apply so directly to my life."

A picture flashes into my head of Ms. Pregent, with her glasses on a chain, and her hair in a bun, telling our class, "If you sleep with someone without a condom, you're also sleeping with everyone they've slept with, and everyone that they've slept with, and so on, and so on ..."

I laugh out loud. "I remember she said the average number of sexual partners a person has is nine, and I was still reeling with the shock of that ..."

"... when she showed us how it multiplied out to 3,917,918," Charlie finishes. "All those years ago, and I'll never forget that number."

"The danger of having a combination health and math teacher."

Charlie looks past me, toward the loft. "I hear you have another high school flashback in your life."

"I mean, not in my life, exactly." Pearson trots out of the barn and drops to his haunches beside me. I lay my hand on his head. "I've seen his dog more than I've seen him."

"What's he doing up there?" Charlie asks.

I shrug. "Beats me. It's not like I can go up and look around, even if I wanted to. Which I don't."

Charlie nods. "Well, I'm glad you don't."

"I definitely don't."

"Are you OK?"

It's a great opportunity to change the subject. "You can report back to Bree that I'm definitely OK." I lay my hand on Abbott's neck. "We're both uninjured, and Abbott was a superstar."

"Hey, I'm just here to deliver sap buckets."

I lift my eyebrows. "Conveniently half-an-hour after I texted Bree to say I was starting Abbott on the drag?"

Charlie grins. "She might have mentioned something."

"She takes good care of me."

Charlie looks at the loft again, then back at me. "Yeah, well, that's what friends are for."

All of a sudden, the two metres seems more like two hundred massive metres keeping me on the outside of the bubble of the only family I really have, and the only people I deeply trust.

The longing to step forward and hug, and be hugged is overwhelming. I bite my lip, and spread the fingers of my right hand through Abbott's mane, scratch Pearson's ear with my left. *Three-million-nine-hundred-and-seventeen thousand-nine-hundred-and-eighteen*, I remind myself, and that gives me the resolve to push a smile into my voice and say, "Well, thanks for coming by. Have a great evening!"

As I walk Abbott into the barn, I wave at the retreating truck and think how Dob might have been right up the stairs the whole time, but I didn't feel safe about starting with Abbott until I texted Bree.

Then I think of her sending Charlie over, and of him coming, and think that's exactly why. Trust is a hard thing to earn, and an easy thing to lose, and I know who I trust.

Six

I don't consider my kitchen to be small, but when filled with drying sap buckets it does look quite crowded.

"I guess we need to take these out of here before I can make breakfast," I tell Pearson who gives me a one-eyebrow-up-one-down look.

"Hey, listen, you got to sleep upstairs since your spot was covered with buckets, so don't you complain."

I stack the clean buckets and place them, upside-down, on the bench outside the kitchen door then go back in to rustle up some food for me and the dog.

***

There's a lot to get done today, so I get out early – whipping through the barn, then riding Lemon and ponying Mocha on a somewhat abbreviated conditioning outing.

By the time I'm done the sun's higher and stronger than it has been so far this spring, and I'm sweating in my long-sleeved black zip-necked top. I go in to switch it for a lighter shirt and when I come out Dob's standing at the edge of the walkway.

I pause in the doorway while my eyes adjust to the sudden brightness. Pearson drops to his haunches beside me.

"So, you still have my dog." Dob whistles. The dog leans into my leg.

I shrug. Turn my hands palms up. *Nothing I can do about it if the dog likes me more.*

"What are those?" Dob juts his chin toward the stacks of buckets.

"How long have you been away?"

"Oh my god, you talked to me."

I give him a second shrug. "Nobody's perfect." *But I'll try harder.*

He looks back at the buckets. "Obviously I know what they are, but what do you have them for?"

I mean, honestly, when he gives me openings like that it's tempting to break my silence but I'm actually finding the whole not-talking thing surprisingly satisfying. Judging by the furrow in Dob's brow it's bugging him, so that works for me.

Besides, Cleo's on her way up the driveway; I can talk to her.

I hope Dob will leave when she arrives. I don't really want to have to socially distantly introduce Cleo to a person I'm not speaking to, and who, in my opinion, there's no need for her to know.

She stops several metres from Dob. Pearson jumps up and runs to her, tail wagging. The look on Dob's face is a picture.

Cleo scratches Pearson's ears, while looking at me. "You ready?"

I brush my hands together. "Let's tap those trees!"

Cleo beams. "Excellent! Let's get started – we have a ton to do."

"I can help."

Cleo's eyes slide sideways to Dob, while I shake my head.

I can see what she's thinking – he's apparently able-bodied and we do have a lot of work to do. I'm not even saying she's wrong. "Why don't you want him to help?" she asks. "Because he broke your heart?"

Ah ... so I guess she does know who he is. "Cleo?"

"Yes?"

"Do you remember when you had a crush on Dexter McNaughton and I didn't tell anybody because I knew it would embarrass you?"

Dob makes a funny snorting sound. "Is that Mitch McNaughton's son? I can't imagine having a crush on a McNaughton."

Cleo and I both turn to him at the same time. "Shut up." To which Cleo adds, "He has more meat on his bones than you."

Dob's looking down at his bony hips when I say – more to the air than to him – "I slept with Mitch McNaughton."

They both say, "You what?" To which Dob adds, "When?"

"I'm guessing after you broke her heart," Cleo says.

I narrow my eyes at her. "He didn't break my heart."

Cleo waves her arms. "Whatever. I don't really want to talk about the love lives ... or sex lives of nearly middle-aged people. I want to get to work."

"About that ..." I say.

"Yes?"

"I'm afraid we might have a fundamental problem."

"What's that?"

I wave toward the woodlot. "I have no idea which of those trees are maples."

Cleo grins. "Ah ... but you're not Sam."

"What do you mean?"

"Grab an armful of buckets and come with me."

***

In the end Dob comes with us too, simply because there's exactly one stack of buckets left over after Cleo and I each take as many as we can carry, and it's easy to let him scoop those up and follow us.

We string out with Cleo in the lead, followed by me, then Dob, until he puts on a burst of speed and runs up beside me. "You didn't seriously sleep with Mitch McNaughton, did you?"

Something flares in me, but it's still not the anger I've been waiting for. It's more like annoyance – like when my hands are full working with the horses, and I get bitten by a mosquito, and I really want to reach out and slap it. In this case my hands are full of sap buckets, and my mind had moved well on past the Mitch McNaughton conversation, and Dob bringing it up again is like the whine of a mosquito in my ear.

Except what I hear instead is the buzz of my phone. Normally I wouldn't answer it, but it seems like the perfect excuse to ignore Dob, so I juggle the buckets onto my left hip and use my right hand to pull my phone out of my pocket. John's smiling face beams out at me from a picture I took last summer with that perfect view from the cabin's front porch behind him. It's very tempting to answer with a sexy "Hey, you ..." and to flirt shamelessly, and to make sure Dob can hear the whole thing.

But ... that's not fair. John's not a toy, or a convenience. He's a nice person who's helped me whenever he can, and who's always been willing to come to the island at a moment's notice, and who – on the two occasions when I finally agreed to a quick overnight in Toronto – gamely passed up tickets to the Leafs, and gala ball evenings to take me to the racetrack, and to spend the entire day at the winter fair with me.

No matter how tempting it is, I'm not going to lead him on now just to make Dob jealous.

I tuck the phone back in my pocket. I'll message him later.

Up ahead Bree's coming out of the woods. She grins at Cleo. "Hi baby!" beams at me, "Hey you!" then the smile drops from her face as she catches sight of Dob. "It's OK," I say. "Ignore him. We're just using him for his body."

Her smile blooms again. "Well, in that case it's too bad there isn't a little more to it. Boy hasn't filled out at all since he left, has he?"

"I'm pretty sure body shaming is wrong," Dob says.

Bree ignores him. "I'm on my way to the cabin," she tells me. "Doing some final measurements, putting my plan in place." She taps the side of her head and winks at me, and I think if nothing else comes out of her reno efforts, at least they'll make her happy. "By the end of the day I'll leave some paint in the main room. If you can get it done by Friday, I can spend Saturday getting everything pulled together."

"Friday, huh? I'll have to check my calendar ... oh, wait, it's completely empty ..."

Bree laughs. "Oh, I can't wait! This is going to be awesome."

She heads off and Dob says, "I don't suppose it's worth me asking what that's all about?"

Cleo answers for me. "I wouldn't bother if I was you. Oh! There's Sam!"

I knew Sam had a photographic memory, but I didn't know it applied to trees. We have to find thirty maple trees, each big enough to be tapped, and "ideally, as close as possible to the path," Cleo tells her uncle.

Cleo's brought a big piece of chalk and we trail Sam with her making big X marks whenever he points out a tree.

Dob follows along as well, and when we've marked thirty trees, he squints up at the bare branches, "How can you be sure they're all maples?"

Cleo wrinkles her nose at him, then holds her phone up for me to see a picture, taken in the fall, at the exact spot where we're standing. Cleo and Bix are standing at the foot of a flaming red maple, and there are two more orangey ones flanking it. All three of those now-bare trees have big chalk Xs on them.

"Good enough for me!" I say.

Like most projects, it seems straightforward to simply drill and tap thirty trees. It's not like there's actual construction involved. But, like most projects, it takes much longer than expected. Sam goes to help Joel in the fields, and Dob gets tired of being given the cold shoulder, which leaves me and Cleo, muddling through.

Cleo says, "The next time we do this ..." half-a-dozen times, to do with things like making sure there are multiple extra batteries charged for the drill, and having a wagon we can pile all the buckets on to pull along with us, and bringing food.

The final time she says it – "The next time we do this, we should tap a few of these trees in more than one spot ..." – I say, "Given how much longer this took than we thought, and how starving you are, are you sure you'll want to do it again?"

She gasps. "Oh, Aspen! How dare you? Come with me."

I follow her back along the path, through the insulated bubble of the woods, to the first trees we tapped, which now seems like a really long time ago. She walks over to the first tree Sam pointed out and beckons me to stand on the other side of the bucket from her. "Lift the lid."

The bottom of the bucket is covered with a thin, clear liquid that simultaneously looks like water, and looks like magic. "Sap!" I breathe.

She nods. "Uh-huh. And watch ..." Even as she points at it, a drop rolls out of the spile and plinks into the bucket.

I meet her eyes. "Yeah, when you put it like that, how could we not do it again?"

She laughs. "And that's before we even taste the maple syrup!"

"So, what now?"

"Now, we let the trees do their thing. Meet back here tomorrow for our first sap collection?"

"You bet." My phone vibrates and I check it. "You'll have to forgive me if I'm bleary-eyed though; looks like my evening might be accounted for." I hold up my phone to show her the text from Bree. **Got Joel to drop off two cans of paint along with drop sheets and all the painting stuff you'll need. It's ready when you are ...**

"Ah, a hot date, then."

I give her a lopsided grin. "Yeah, I don't expect I'll get a better offer."

Cleo nods, and for an uncharacteristic fleeting second her face goes serious. "Trust yourself to find someone you can trust," she tells me.

"Whoa," I say. "Where did you get those wise words from?"

She blinks. "You. When Dexter called me two hours before the dance and I asked you if I should skip my 4H meeting to go with him ..."

"... and the next day you found out Julia Montgomery dumped him two hours before the dance ..."

She nods. "Thank god I didn't miss that 4H meeting. That was the one where we decided to do the fund-raising for the Winter Fair trip."

I point at the sap bucket. "And now you're on your way."

* * *

I've eaten, and changed into the one set of clothing I own that qualifies as worse-than-barn-clothes, and I'm heading to the cabin with Pearson by my side, a bottle of Diet Coke, a portable Bluetooth speaker, and a heart full of optimism. I'm sure I'll be sick of painting by the time the sun's setting, but for now the joy of seeing the first sap fill our first bucket, and the opportunity to make the cabin even better are driving me forward. I figure if I get a good start, I can ride it through even when I'm paint-splattered, and the endless motion of the roller is making me cross-eyed.

I climb the front steps to the cabin, pause on the front porch and take a minute to appreciate the view. It really is stand-out.

I bring up my contact picture of John and hold it up to the real thing. Hard to believe but this picture proves the view will be even prettier come July.

I wonder if I'll have guests by then. I wonder how the world will be.

Pearson whines.

I could stand here and wonder all day, but I can see the paint cans through the window.

"Come on then."

I let the dog in, then take a step back, into the corner of the unpainted room, snap a photo, and send it to John, captioned. **Before.**

Then I roll up my sleeves. "Let's get to work," I tell the dog.

Seven

The day doesn't so much dawn, as it slowly lightens from pitch black, through deep, grainy grey, to a sort of dull half-light that takes us two steps back toward winter from yesterday's big step forward toward summer.

While I wash my breakfast dishes, the radio tells me twice as many people have already died in New York as died in 9-11, cases in Canada are accelerating, Toronto is our epicentre, and the stock markets are predicted to open on a steep downslide.

Great.

Why did I even have that on in the first place?

When I step into the barn, the cat's left an eviscerated mouse spread-eagled on the concrete floor. Pearson sniffs at it and steps delicately around it.

When I close the gate behind the horses, the latch won't close. I have to trudge back to the barn to get a lead rope to tie it shut.

Lemon and Mocha are both scheduled for dressage schooling today.

I ride Mocha in the nicely furrowed sand ring only to discover that sometime since her last dressage school she seems to have lost the ability to bend right. Or, at least, that's what she wants me to believe.

When I go to bring Lemon in for her ride, Campbell wanders over to see me. I pat her dark shoulder, which is strangely sticky. "What have you gotten yourself into?"

I run my hand farther up her neck under her long mane. It comes back coated red in tacky blood.

I freeze, my heart races. *Oh-my-god, oh-my-god, oh-my-god* ... I need the vet. I need my phone. I need help.

This mare ... she belongs here more than I do. She was my aunt's favourite. She owns the fields. She leads the other horses. She anchors me.

Nothing can happen to her.

Desperate times.

"Dob!"

Campbell who, to do her credit, is completely calm, flicks her ear at me. "Sorry," I whisper and cover her ear, then use all the air in my lungs to scream, "Dob!!!"

The loft door opens and he's standing there, barefoot as usual, blinking, asking "Is the barn on fire?"

I seem to have found some more air. "You never joke about a barn being on fire. *Ever.* For the love of god would you put some shoes on and come down here. Now!"

He squints into the bright morning. "Are you covered in blood?"

"Hurry!"

To be fair, by the time I snap the lead I brought for Lemon onto Campbell's halter, and lead her to the yard in front of the barn doors, Dob is there, with shoes on. "What's going on?"

"Hold her." I long-arm the lead in his direction, which keeps us more or less six feet apart. "I'll be right back."

In the tack room I grab my phone, then start picking up everything and anything I can think of. I run warm water into a clean bucket. Throw a new sponge in. Shrug the extension cord onto my shoulder and shove the clippers into my back pocket.

I burst out of the barn to find Dob standing at the end of the lead, staring at Campbell, who's in turn, staring at him. "Really?"

"What?"

"No wonder your dog doesn't love you."

"What do you mean?"

"You don't have to socially distance from horses, you know ... forget it. She's calm enough for now, but you'll need to hold her more closely when I clean the cut."

I braid a chunk of her mane to the far side of her neck, which reveals a blood-matted mess. "Not that helpful ..." I look at Dob. "OK, this is go-time. I'm going to have to take my chances being within two metres of your supposed-to-be-quarantine self, because I need you to hold her right under her chin, like this." I take a hold of the clip where it attaches to her halter.

"Um ..."

"What?"

"I just ... I'm not sure how good I'll be at this. I don't know much about horses."

I exhale, blowing my hair away from my face. "She should be fine – she's very sensible – but part of keeping her fine is her believing you're there for her. If you're standing way over there, that's not reassuring for her. Besides ..."

"Besides, what?"

I hold my arms wide to indicate the wide-open space around us. "Besides, I don't have a choice."

"OK, well since I'm your last resort."

I squeeze about half the water out of the sponge. "Dob?"

"Yes?"

"Now would be good."

"Oh." He takes a visible inhale and steps forward, putting his hand about a foot away from the clip. "There."

"No." I shake my head. "Here. Put your hand where mine is."

He slides his hand up against mine and for the first time in years, our skin touches. His possibly virus-ridden, and mine, tacky with blood. *Romantic.* I'm glad there's no jolt of electricity, no flutter of nerves. Campbell needs, and deserves all my attention right now. Thank goodness my head's overriding my heart.

"Alright, here goes."

Sure enough, Campbell is a rock-solid star. She stands quietly while I squeeze water over the cut until it – mostly – runs away clear.

I touch my fingers lightly to the skin around the cut.

"What do you think?" Dob asks.

I shake my head. "I'm still not sure. Her coat's really thick – I need to shave it."

"Is she going to like that?"

I look at him. "I've never known the clippers to send her jumping out of her skin, if that's what you're asking."

"That wasn't exactly what I was asking ..."

I wink, and flick the clippers to "on" and their buzzing drones out the rest of his sentence.

Campbell is very good about the clippers as well. I try not to go too close to the edges of the cut, but it's hard to see them, and I do have to shave near enough to give a clear view, so she flinches once or twice. I look over at Dob and he's very white. When I turn the clippers off he swallows hard. "I have to admit something."

"What?"

"I'm afraid of horses."

I lift my eyebrows. "Really? Seriously?"

He nods.

"And all those years I thought you were being a complete jerk when you'd stand in the doorway of the barn and refuse to help me."

"Well, I guess it was a pretty jerky way to handle it."

"How did I never know that?"

He shrugs. "It was easier to cover it up by giving you a hard time than to muster up the maturity or trust to tell you."

"Hmm ..." A breeze slips across my skin. The sun warms my back. I scratch Campbell's withers and she shifts her weight and sighs. I give Dob the first genuine smile since he arrived. "Well, thanks for trusting me enough to tell me now."

"I'm not sure I was hiding it very well."

"I did wonder if you were going to faint for a minute there."

He places a tentative hand on Campbell's face. "Well at least I made it through the hard part."

"I hate to tell you this, but I don't think that was the hard part. I'm fairly sure she's going to need stitches."

***

She needs stitches.

After I've shown Dr. Lucent Campbell's shaved neck, she says, "I think she'll be OK no matter what, but I also think the cut would heal better with a couple of sutures."

This mare was my aunt's favourite. This mare deserves the best. "That's fine. I'll pay for you to come."

There's a hesitation on the line that makes me look at Dob, that makes us both raise our eyebrows. "The thing is, I was at a conference in Chicago last week. I'm in self-isolation." Before I can ask, she says. "I do have a colleague covering my emergencies, but we're talking major emergencies."

"So not 'my mare needs a couple of quick sutures?'"

She laughs. "No. Not that. You can do it, though."

"I ... what?"

"I'd recommend two or three interrupted sutures. That means each one is separate – they don't even connect to each other. You put them in, tie them off and, voila – after you make sure the cut's absolutely clean, of course."

"Dr. Lucent ..."

"Aspen, this is exactly why I sold you that enhanced first-aid kit. It has everything you need to do this, including topical anaesthetic. I'll talk you through it."

I look at Dob and mouth, *'I can't.'*

He holds my eyes. "You can."

"No."

"OK, then. I'll do it."

"What? No. You're afraid of horses. You're not doing it. I'll do it."

"See? I *knew* you could do it."

"Hello?" It's Dr. Lucent's, slightly removed voice. "Is somebody doing this?"

"I am." As soon as I say it every single butterfly I didn't feel when my hand touched Dob's begins crashing around in my gut.

"Great!" Dr. Lucent says. "Now get the first aid kit and show me what's in it and we'll go from there."

***

With Campbell back in the field sporting three neat sutures liberally smeared with ointment to keep out any spring mud, I'm relieved, pleased with myself, and I'm feeling kindly toward Dob.

So kindly that I'm making him a grilled cheese sandwich, with bacon in it, as a thank you.

When it's ready I carry a tray over to the loft stairs, I leave my plate near the bottom and place the rest of the tray on the landing, several steps above mine.

He comes out shaking his just-washed hands, sits on a tread, and picks up half of the sandwich. "Smells good. I'm hungry."

"Must be the aftermath of being completely terrified, because I'm starving, too."

"In my non-expert opinion, you did a great job on those sutures."

I shrug. "When it came right down to it, it wasn't hugely different from sewing up the tears the horses make in their blankets every winter. Also, doing it myself saved me a fair bit of money."

"Speaking of money, the loft is really nice. You should charge more."

"You're already paying extra. I should thank you for that." I force myself to meet his eyes. "I'm sorry. I'm normally a good host, and I've been juvenile about you being here. It was uncalled-for."

He shakes his head. "I was unrealistic. The news kept getting worse and worse, and I could see there was a shutdown coming, and I had this overwhelming need to be home. I'd been thinking about it for a while anyway, so it seemed like the right time to finally do it."

"That makes sense. When all the stories kept coming in about people trapped away from home, I was really glad I was here. Why should you feel any differently?"

We're both quiet for a minute, while a stray goose honks overhead toward the river, and the breeze flutters the laundry on the clothesline behind the house, and Lemon squeals at Mocha for invading her personal space.

Dob clears his throat. "I like that we're talking."

I nod. "It's definitely better. More mature."

"There's something else I should tell you."

"Which is?"

"I lied."

I snort. "Is that news?" Then I hold up my hand. "Sorry. Sorry. Not mature. It's too easy to revert. I'll let you speak."

"I didn't come through the States."

"I knew that. Or," I clarify, "I knew you didn't come on the New York ferry, which made it safe to assume you didn't come through New York at all, because what would be the point?"

He stares at me. His mouth is actually hanging open.

"Come on, Dob. How many times did we get phone calls back before we had our licenses, warning us not to drive because the police had come over on the ferry? Have you forgotten the island gossip machine? The minute you got on the main ferry it was only a – short – matter of time before I heard about it." I pause. "What I couldn't figure out is why you'd bother lying about it."

He pinches the final crumbs of his sandwich off his plate. "I've changed."

I blink. Bite my tongue. Force myself to stay quiet.

"Which I know is easy to say ... and that's the point. I figured I needed a while to show you. Fourteen days sounded like a good start, and if I said I was in the States you'd have to give me fourteen days. And see? Maybe I was right because it's already been what – five days – and we're just finally talking now."

He rubs his hand across his forehead (*don't touch your face!*). "I thought I knew exactly what to say, and now I don't, other than, I know what I did was unforgiveable. I know I left you in the lurch. I'm here now because I want to be, and I'm really hoping ... well ... this is an awesome start." He locks eyes with me and grins, and recognition stirs deep in me.

That grin. It was what made people notice Dob. And like him. When he grinned at me that way I knew he'd done something wrong ... and was usually already on my way to forgiving him.

Seeing that grin brings it home to me that Dob is really sitting here, in front of me. That what I've been waiting for all these years has happened. He's back. I knew he'd come back, and he did.

"So ...?"

I shake my head. "Sorry. What was that?"

"I'm wondering what you think."

I think this is not the way I expected to feel. I think the way Dob bought his fourteen days to prove how much he's changed, was by telling me another lie. I think, if I parse his speech, he never actually said he was sorry for taking off the way he did.

I'm not ready to say any of that, though. I'm not ready to say anything.

The person who's been there for me all these years, the person who never lets me down, the person who's saved me more times than I can count, saves me again. Bree's text jitters onto my phone. **Hey you, fancy a walk? Meet me at the end of the driveway?**

I smile back at Dob and wave my phone in his direction. "I think I have to go."

Then I reply to Bree. **God, yes. Perfect timing.**

***

The inner workings of my brain, churning through Dob's speech, and his latest lie, and much bigger questions like, *Can a person ever truly change?* switch gears completely when I see Bree's face.

"Oh, hey you – what's up?"

"Bix is sick."

"Oh, Bree ... like how sick?"

She starts walking – fast – and I rush to keep pace with her. Power walking helps Bree cope with stress. "It's just a cold. I think. I'm not *worried*, worried ..."

"But you're a bit worried."

She gives a muffled laugh. "Yeah. It's less the actual fact of him being sick and more that it's somehow brought everything into focus. That we're really in this.

That we're kind of screwed. That if he does get sicker, or if somebody gets hurt out in the fields, that we have to go to a hospital, which kind of seems like the scariest place in the world to go right now."

"Or, I could stitch them up."

"Pardon me?"

"Somebody – and there hasn't been an arrest yet, but Abbott doesn't have shoes on, and he's naturally sweet-natured, so my suspect list is pretty much down to Lemon and Mocha – anyway, Lemon-or-Mocha kicked Campbell, and she lost enough blood to make blood services weep, and I called Dr. Lucent who said Campbell should have stitches ..."

"But isn't Dr. Lucent in self-isolation?"

"Bingo."

"You didn't really ..."

"I really did."

"How?"

"Well, way back when it looked like there might be a ferry strike, I got Dr. Lucent to put together a super-duper first-aid kit for me, so I had lidocaine cream, and a suture kit and everything."

"But, how did you make Campbell stand still? And how did you make yourself ..." Bree makes a scrunched-up face and mimes tugging a needle through flesh.

"Dob held her," I say.

"Well, I'm glad he's proving useful."

"He's proving something ..." I mutter.

"Oh. There's something there. Care to share?"

I shake my head. "Not really. Maybe another time. Suffice it to say, he lied, and told me he took the New York ferry to get on the island ..."

"... but the New York ferry isn't running yet."

I lift my eyebrows.

"Ah, yes. You did say it was a lie."

"And just now he's told me he lied because he wanted to have a chance to show me how much he's changed ..."

"By lying to you?"

I laugh. "Do you actually have a direct line to the inside of my head? Because that's exactly what I've been thinking ... anyway, listen, that's not important. You have a lot going on and we should talk about you."

She grins. "Actually, I'm all good now. I'd much rather worry about kids having colds, than be you, dealing with your recently returned ex-boyfriend who absconded in the dead of night and essentially left you at the altar – even if it wasn't *your* altar. Thanks for the perspective."

"My pleasure. I live to serve. How's everything else?"

"Honestly, it would probably be OK if I could get my hands on a humidifier. It always helps Bix sleep better when he's sick, and our old one conked out after his last cold. I meant to get around to replacing it, and now, of course, it's not like I can easily go out and pick one up."

I snap my fingers. "The online noticeboard."

"Pardon me?"

"Polly Black set it up. Ky told me about it. I checked it out really quickly yesterday. Anyone on the island who needs help or can give help can post there. I bet somebody has a humidifier they can lend you." The card Ky gave me is still in my pocket. I hand it to her.

"You don't need the card?" she asks.

"I bookmarked the site."

"Well, in that case, everything is fine. Let's stop talking about my sick kid."

We walk the big loop up to the highway and back and debate whether it's OK to order non-essential items online right now. "The other day the UPS guy brought me a drugstore order and he said he's fine with delivering that, but he said some woman on the next concession got a Gap order and why does she need that? And I was like, 'Shi-i-it' because I just ordered a new bra."

"Hmm ... maybe if it's an ugly bra – with really thick straps and uncomfortable underwire, in that terrible colour they call 'flesh tone' – maybe then it could be considered essential."

Bree looks down at her tiny chest and we both giggle at the thought of her double As in a heavy-duty brassiere. "It's from Victoria's Secret," she says.

"Then I'm afraid your cover is blown. You're going to have to live with the scorn of the UPS guy."

"Maybe I'll tell him it's for you."

I shake my head. "Absolutely not. Then it will be all over the island that I'm getting raunchy lingerie delivered to the house, and someone will remember Dob's back on the island, and that he's staying at my place … nope, I cannot take the gossip."

"OK. I'll take the hit, because I really don't want you-and-Dob gossip circulating."

"Sounds like there's something more you'd like to say about that."

She sighs. "Charlie's told me not to interfere … and, anyway, isn't that Cleo coming?" Sure enough, as we've been walking back toward my driveway, a figure's been approaching it from the other direction.

"Wait? You and Charlie are talking about me and Dob?"

She waves her hand. "Oh not about you in particular … just in general …"

"I'm not convinced."

She shoots me an overly sweet smile and calls, "Hey Baby!"

Cleo waves and breaks into a jog.

"Did you start on your video for Tech class?" Bree asks her.

"What video?" I ask.

Cleo pulls out her phone and reads off. "This week's assignment is to shoot a two-to-three-minute video showing the things that are making you happy during the pandemic. Please use three different types of shots ... blah, blah, blah." She sighs. "I wish I'd never taken Tech."

"Cleo! You're the happiest person I know."

"That's just it. I'm happy enough without analyzing it. I don't want to have to make a list, and a video."

"Tell you what – I'll also make a list. In solidarity with you."

"And a video?" Cleo asks.

"Nope. I'm not the one taking Tech, but the first thing on my list will be spending time with you ..." I point to Bree, "... and you," I point to Cleo. "See? I'm starting a list on my phone right now and putting you two on it."

"Great idea!" Bree says.

"Does that mean you're going to start one too?" I ask.

"No way. The thing that's making me happy during this pandemic is that I've been let off the hook for organizing duty for Bix's school's silent auction – imagine the lists I would have had to make for that! I support you two in spirit but I'm not giving myself a new list to work on."

"Support in spirit isn't really what I was going for," Cleo says.

"Hmm …well, come to think of it, I know something you might want to add to your video."

"Now?"

I nod. "When we collect the sap."

"Let's go then!" She wiggles her fingers at Bree. "See you for dinner."

Bree, in turn, points her finger at me. "I went by the cabin …"

"And you're about to tell me what a great job I did."

"And, I'm about to say what a great colour I chose for you."

"Bree! You didn't choose the colour. It's leftover from when you painted your master bedroom."

"I still *chose* it … last year, when we painted the bedroom … anyway, what I was going to say is it's a great start. You need to get another coat on there tonight and I can take over."

I salute her. "Yes ma'am. It's not like I have anything else to do."

She lifts her eyebrows and looks down the driveway to the loft. "I certainly hope you don't have anything else to do."

"Are you guys talking about Aspen doing that Dob guy?"

Both Bree and I gasp, "Cleo!"

"I'm not 'doing' Dob!" I say.

"Aspen isn't 'doing' anybody!" Bree adds.

"That's too bad. I mean, not that you're not doing *him*, because ..." Cleo shrugs. "There's something about him I don't like. But it is too bad you're not doing anyone."

Bree claps her hand over Cleo's mouth. "OK, sweet daughter, as much as I might agree with you, I really can't listen to my fourteen-year-old discuss these things."

"Hey," Cleo peels Bree's fingers away. "You weren't able to talk about sex with your mother, and look where that got you."

"Yup. Knocked up at sixteen. See? You and I can talk about sex, but that doesn't mean you should talk about Aspen's sex life."

"Or lack thereof ..." Cleo starts.

"OK," I say. "I'm calling a halt to it now. Come with me or I'll drive Abbott to collect the sap alone."

"Did you say drive?" Cleo asks. "Oh, wow. Forget sex. Can I help you hitch him up? Can I ...?" She's already running up the driveway with the wind whisking her words away.

I reach into the mailbox, pull out a couple of long, white envelopes, and make a face at Bree.

She waves her hand at me. "Don't even read them. Go have fun with my daughter. Become a maple syrup magnate."

I shove them in my back pocket and give her a thumbs-up. "Yes ma'am – will do."

* * *

"I didn't know Abbott was ready for this," Cleo says as she helps me wheel the wagon out of the shed.

"I'm not positive he is. Don't get me wrong – I think he is, and I've done everything I can to make sure he is, but ..."

"There's only one way to find out!"

Once he's hitched to the wagon we stand back for a good look while Abbott cocks his hip and lets his lower lip droop. "I guess it's a good sign that he looks relaxed," I say.

Cleo snaps a picture. "How on earth do you know how to put on the harness and hitch it to the wagon?"

"Honestly, this particular harness is simpler than it looks. There are some really fancy ones in the shed I haven't even touched since Aunt Jean died. But there's no way I could even put this one on if she hadn't taught me while I was growing up."

"And now I can learn from you."

Just like that, I'm hit with the feeling I always thought I'd experience when I saw Dob again. It's like somebody put gratitude, and happiness, and sadness in a blender then sent them all rushing through me at the same time – it aches so I have to push on my breastbone. My eyes sting so I have to blink back tears. But it's not the former love-of-my-life stirring up these feelings in me. It's the presence of this gangly, freckled, pony-tailed girl, combined with the memory of my aunt who bred this horse and taught me how to train him.

I have sympathy for Cleo – I wouldn't begin to know how to capture this moment on video. I make a mental note to add **Teaching Cleo the things Aunt Jean taught me** to my list.

As it turns out, it's Abbott who teaches both of us. He waits, completely patiently, while I climb onto the bench seat and take up the reins, and when I say, "Walk on," he leans into his harness and pulls the wagon as though he was born to it. Which, considering his dam, I guess he was.

Cleo, walking beside him, looks up at me. "He's amazing!"

He really is.

As we get to the end of the driveway, his ears flick back to me. I steer him as far over to the right as I can to give him a nice wide turning circle, then I say, "Haw." He obediently turns left, still with one ear on me. "Keep haw," I tell him. Cleo's there, with her hand out, ready to guide him, but there's no need. After all, he and I have done this a dozen times with the long lines.

I laugh. "It's like he's saying 'I know how this goes. So, I have a wagon behind me – so what?'"

"He is really clever – aren't you? Aren't you the clever boy?"

I tell him to "whoa" and he stops square, and I say. "Your turn."

"I get to drive him?"

"Why not? He's a pro. He'll teach you everything you need to know."

We switch places and I walk back the length of the drive by Abbott's shoulder, but he and Cleo don't need me. She asks him to halt by the barn, and he does, and she says, "Now what?"

"Now, I would say, we grab a big container and Abbott can pull the wagon through the woodlot so we can collect the sap."

It's as magical as it sounds. The sun dribbling filtered by the evergreens, splashing through spots where the other trees don't yet have their leaves. The twitter of early season songbirds. The background rat-a-tat of a woodpecker. An incessant background hum of wind, and water birds, honking and re-arranging themselves in the sweep of the bay.

Abbott's footfalls are muffled by the carpet of last season's leaves and browned-off pine needles. The only other sounds he makes are an occasional squeak from the wagon, a soft clink-jingle of harness, and the occasional deep snorts he gives when we tell him how good he is.

I know all over the world there are people missing nightclubs, and evenings at the theatre, and the ability to get on a plane and fly across time zones, but this, for me, is perfection. I'm almost embarrassed to admit the pandemic has brought me riches I wouldn't have had otherwise.

Cleo's tongue sticks out the corner of her mouth as she concentrates on getting every drop of sap from one of the buckets into the first of the two 15-litre water containers we've brought. "I can't believe how much sap we have already!"

"Maybe we'll raise enough money to get you to the Winter Fair after all."

"Oh, yeah – I forgot to tell you – we're having a virtual 4H meeting tonight. Everybody thinks we should give the money we raise to charity, instead of saving for the trip."

"Cleo ..." I start, then find I don't have the breath or composure to continue. This has happened to me before – I've been dealing with a big thing, then some small thing comes in and undoes me.

It happened after my aunt died. I knew she was going to die. She knew she was going to die. We planned her memorial out together. We even planned her death out, in that she wanted to be comfortable, and at home.

There was a brief lull of peace, and of relief at managing to keep her at home, and comfortable, then the whirlwind hit. All the execution of all the planning. The legal stuff, the money stuff, the horse stuff, the basic-everyday stuff ... I thought I was coping. Thought I wasn't overwhelmed by grief because I was prepared for her death.

Then, one day I got back from a trip to the lawyer, and the bank, and the funeral home, and on my doorstep was a container full of fresh-cut vegetables and dip. There was a note saying, (h) I expect you've been given a lot of casseroles, but there's only so much lasagna a person can eat. I thought you might like these. (h).

It was from the woman who runs the bakery in the village. Despite never having been a particular friend to either me, or my aunt, it was her kind gesture that brought me literally to my knees. Bent over, sobbing on the step outside the kitchen door, with the cold of the stone seeping through my jeans, realizing the grief was just beginning to flow.

"Aspen?" Cleo asks. "Don't you think it's a good idea?"

"Cleo, I'm completely overwhelmed with what an amazing idea it is."

She shrugs. "I mean, let's face it, the way things are going, there's a good chance the fair will be canceled anyway, and lots of people are having a much harder time; I figure it's the least I can do."

I concentrate hard on breathing. On not crying. On not-freaking-the-fourteen-year-old-out. "Well, the least I can do is make a donation. Let me know when you have the page set up."

"Excellent!" Cleo claps. "I've got a donation before I've even started."

I hold my hand up. "I have to warn you, it won't be that much."

"Oh, it doesn't matter. Once I have one donation, other people will donate, too. For now, you can donate your time by taking Abbott out and turning him around so I can get solid video of him coming toward me along the path."

"That, I can do."

Eight

When I bring Abbott back from his first day as a real working horse, I give him an extra neck scratch, and a small scoop of sweetfeed. "Shhh ... don't tell the ladies," I tell him.

I give him time to eat it while I clean and organize the harness, then I bring the mares in.

"Everybody's in early tonight because Momma's going painting," I tell them.

They don't care. They're antsy, dancing in their stalls and whickering aggressively until I bring them each a flake or two of hay, then everybody settles into a corner of their stall; all their heads go down and the barn fills with the sound of munching horses. My job is to bring them hay and I've done that. They don't care if I'm going skydiving next – as long as I'm back to feed them in the morning.

Still, talking to them makes me happy.

I pull out my phone and thumb it in to my happiness list: **Talking to my horses.**

Then, before I can get distracted, or lose momentum – while Cleo's example is still strong in my mind, and my heart – I go to Polly's island noticeboard and post. **Offering: free indoor or outdoor board for one or two horses. If you need help caring for your horse(s) during the pandemic please contact me to make arrangements.**

On the one hand it's scary to have made the posting. On the other hand, it truly does feel like the very least I can do under the circumstances.

Pearson, who I've become used to as a constant background presence, trots over and drops his hind end onto my toes, then looks up at me with a big whine. "You're right," I tell him. "I need to get over myself. What's the big deal about offering to look after one more horse?" Then I add, **The dog I never knew I needed** to my list.

I snap my fingers at him. "Come on. I'll give you some food while I get ready for painting, then you can come keep me company."

I'm running through the list in my head: feed Pearson, change into yesterday's painting clothes, bring lots of snacks, when I stop dead in front of my kitchen door.

There's a hand-written note stuck on it.

I recognize the writing. It used to appear on the list on my refrigerator – (h) Toothpaste, Half-and-half cream,

Double Stuf Oreos (h). It was – sometimes – on cards I – sometimes – received for my birthday, Valentine's Day, Easter. When Dob remembered. It was hand-writing I really, really wanted to see somewhere ... anywhere ... after he left. I looked all over our apartment – on the magnetic notepad on our refrigerator, on my bedside table, under my pillow, under his – wanting to see something that explained, (h) I had to go because ... (h), (h) I'll be back soon ... (h), even (h) I stopped loving you and I was too scared to tell you in person. (h) That would have been better than nothing at all.

Pearson scratches at my leg. Lightly. A gentle reminder.

"Yes, you're right. I did promise to feed you. Come on in and I'll do that."

With the dog rattling the kibble around in his dish, I stand in front of the kitchen counter and look at Dob's note by my left-hand, and the bills I collected from the mailbox by my right.

I can ratchet up my anxiety level by opening the bills. I can be overwhelmed by the news on the radio of more deaths, more job losses, more declarations of states of emergency.

I unfold Dob's note. It's got to be less upsetting than the other two. I hope.

(h) Aspen. I've owed you this note for a long, long time. Every time I thought about it, it seemed impossible to start.

As crazy as this sounds, dropping everything, and driving across the country actually seemed easier than dealing with the past. I know this pandemic has been terrible for a lot of people, but to me it felt like an opportunity for a fresh start.

After our conversation this afternoon, I hope you think so too.

Nothing is the same. Things in the world won't ever be the way they were before. Success will be in letting some things go – letting the past be water under the bridge – and moving forward. I would love to move forward with you, and I wonder how you feel about it?

As a start, maybe I could repay some of your hospitality by making you dinner tonight? With Double Stuf Oreos for dessert, of course ... (h)

I stare out the window. I watch a fox slink across the field halfway down to the water. I think in this crazy new world, the only thing I know for sure is that in a few weeks the grass will be so high I won't be able to see the fox.

I try to imagine what my life will look like in a few weeks. Which, of course, is impossible to predict. Instead, I try to picture what I'd like it to look like.

Pearson nudges my elbow and I pull out my phone and add **Pearson's cold nose** to my happiness list. I look at Dob's note again. The note I've waited four years for. I look at Dob's scribbled signature at the bottom.

I put my phone away, and make an extra-thick peanut-butter-and-jam sandwich, then I change into my painting clothes and head to the cabin.

***

There's a light that only comes on the island, that reminds you this is a place like no other.

It comes mostly in the early mornings and evenings, when shadows are unusually long, and clouds hang low, and I'd be hard pressed to describe it to anyone who hasn't seen it other than to say it looks like a filter's been applied to the whole world; atmospheric but still absolutely clear.

That light fills the field as I traipse across it with Pearson leaping back and forth in front of me. It fills me so full of gratitude that it pushes out the guilt I initially felt at ignoring Dob's note.

Just because he wrote it, doesn't mean I have to jump to respond.

He's had four years to think about things. I'm entitled to a few hours.

As soon as I start dwelling on it again, I lift my eyes to the cabin and notice how snug and sweet it looks with the towering evergreens behind it, and how the steps leading up to the front door beg to be sat on, so that's where I sit to eat my sandwich before I go in and tackle Bree's mandated second coat.

As I'm finishing my last bite, and Pearson's working on the finger full of peanut butter I offered him, my phone rings.

Nope. Not dealing with it.

Except, what if it's Bree to tell me Bix took a turn for the worse? Or Cleo with an important maple syrup update, or Agatha responding to my latest update on Lemon and Mocha?

I'll check. If it's Dob I'm not answering.

It's John.

Oh.

I remember another evening, suffused with island light, when I was also painting – except that time it was the trim on the outside of the big picture window – while John cut boards to replace the past-their-expiry-date and, quite frankly, dangerous ones on the porch stairs. In fact, it's one of those new boards I'm sitting on right now.

The memory makes me happy, and because I'm supposed to fill my life with things that make me happy, I answer. "Hey!"

"Hi! I didn't expect to catch you."

"This is pretty much where I am these days."

"Lucky you."

"Where are you?"

"Home. In my room, actually, with the door shut because Dennis is having a Zoom cocktail party in the living room."

I scan the wide-open space around me. "Yeah, must be tough to be socially distancing with a roommate in a ... how big is your condo?"

"Eight hundred square feet."

"Squishy. It must actually be a bit of a relief to go to the office."

"Oh, that's over. Only the people on the daily press briefing are still going in. So, the Premier and whichever cabinet minister is talking with him. The rest of us are working from home."

"Oh, my goodness. And you don't even have a balcony ..."

"Nope. But I'm also not a social butterfly. It's much tougher for Dennis. More importantly, though, how are you? What have you been doing?"

"Quite a lot, actually. I'm afraid I'd talk your ear off if I told you everything."

"Aspen, I'm locked in my ten-foot by twelve-foot bedroom. Talk away."

"Honestly, John, it's not that interesting. It's farm stuff."

"You have no idea how interesting that sounds to me right now."

"I ..." I've stepped into the cabin and am looking at the vast expanse of wall I have to paint before I can go to bed. But ... I also like the thought of talking to a human being I'm not actually living with on this island. "How would you feel about me talking while I paint?"

"I feel like the only way that could be better would be if I could have a roller and be there, too."

"OK, let me get set up and I'll ping you back on speaker phone."

Bree was right that the second coat makes all the difference. Her very expensive, clay-based, so-natural-you-could-drink-it paint rolls on like a dream. As the sun lowers it hits the first wall I did, where the paint is already drying, and shows me how great the finished product is going to look.

And with the swish-swoosh-swoop of the roller in the background, I talk to John. I tell him about Abbott pulling the wagon. About Bree, and her vision for the cabin. About Campbell, and the gory gouge on her neck and how I sewed it up.

"I can't believe you did that!" he says. "Can you send me a picture of the stitches?"

He doesn't ask who held her for me, and I don't tell him.

I tell him about the island notice board, and the cool and creative things people are doing to help other people get through. "The first five spots in every ferry line-up are reserved for healthcare workers," I say, "And there's a mailbox on the dock where people who need help can put their grocery lists, and if you're going over, you grab somebody's list and shop for them, and drop their food off on your way home. And Cleo ... oh wait, I didn't tell you about our maple syrup, did I?"

I move to my final stretch of wall. "... so, anyway, she was going to put whatever we make from selling maple syrup into her fundraising page to go to the Winter Fair, but now her whole 4H group has decided to donate the funds to charity instead ..." There's a flutter of deeper dark against the falling night beyond the window – a bat, most likely – and I look to see nothing left of the day's light but a gleam along the horizon. "Whoa, John, I just realized how late it is – I can't believe you've listened to all this."

"I can't believe how busy you've been."

I shrug, then remember of course he can't hear my shrug. "It's better than the alternative."

I consider telling him about my happiness list, then I'm afraid it'll make me sound stupid, then I think about having courage and about what courage means.

"I've been keeping this list. Of things that make me happy."

I wait for him to make fun of me. To wisecrack – *"Am I on it a hundred times?"* He says, "That's a really good idea. Do you want to tell me any of the things on it?"

There's a blister in the vee between my thumb and index finger, and my cheeks are tight with dried paint splatter, but I just have a final strip of wall left and my near-finish is making me giddy. "Having lots of toilet paper!" I laugh.

"That's a good one."

"And the horses."

"Of course."

"No more pre-dawn supply teaching calls."

"I can think of better things to do in the pre-dawn."

"Whoa ... I'm blushing." And it's true. My paint-speckled cheeks are hot as I remember one particular July morning when John woke me up and we pressed our bodies together while the songbirds came to life outside and the breeze luffed the curtains into the half-lit bedroom.

We're both quiet for a second, then I finally say, "You should see this place. It looks great."

"Now that would go on a list of things that would make me happy."

"I'll send pictures when it's all dry and Bree's worked her home decor magic."

"Please do."

Pearson gives a yawn that turns into a whine and I say, "Oh, the dog's telling me it's time to go."

As soon as the words are out of my mouth, I freeze. *Shit. Dog.*

"Dog? Since when do you have a dog?"

I don't want to tell him.

Why don't I want to tell him? It would be easy to say it's because I don't want to discuss one guy I've slept with, with another guy I've slept with, but I don't think it's entirely that.

It's something deeper.

I'm ashamed.

The thought of Dob embarrasses me. The realization that I've been keeping an important part of my life on hold all these years while I've waited for him.

And now that he's back ... well, he's just a guy. What does it say about me that I chose to hold on for somebody who left me in the worst possible way, instead of moving on with somebody new?

It confirms I'm a coward. And, since he doesn't seem to have figured that out, I don't particularly want John to know.

But maybe if I was brave I'd tell him?

I have no idea.

"It's a long story." I don't get a gold star for bravery, but at least it's true.

"Hmm ... well, I think that's good. I've always been able to picture a dog there."

I look over at Pearson. "He's a great dog."

There's another silence and John says, "And you should go take care of the dog."

"I should."

"OK, well thanks for helping me survive my banishment from the Zoom cocktail party."

"Anytime."

"Bye, Aspen."

Good-bye. It's the next thing to say. It would be perfectly fine. But it wouldn't be brave.

I take a deep breath and say, "I'm adding something."

"You're what?"

"I'm adding a new thing to my list. Two-hour social distancing phone calls."

"Your happiness list? I made it?" He sounds really happy.

Hung-up-on-Dob, afraid-to-move-forward, cowardly me would say. *"Well, the phone call made it."*

Sutured-my-horse, making-maple-syrup, surviving-a-pandemic-one-day-at-a-time me says, "Absolutely. I'm putting you right at the top."

Nine

I've seen the jokes about people losing track of the days. With no offices to go to, no school in session, and the news pretty much the same every day – this many more cases, this many more deaths, this huge event-that's-never-been-canceled-before-canceled – no wonder people are posting things like, **Until further notice the days of the week are now called thisday, thatday, otherday, someday, yesterday, today and nextday.**

Then it happens to me. After my frantic push to paint the cabin, I lose a couple of days. The things I accomplish in those days are the things that have to get done every day, no matter what – the bare basics.

The horses get fed, and exercised. I feed myself, and Pearson. I start a shopping list, because clearly one of these days I'm going to have to go back to the grocery store. I'll do that anotherday. I should add that one to the list.

Bix gets sicker. **Not to the point that I'm worried about him,** Bree texts, although I suspect she is, **but enough that he can't entertain himself, and I'm on call all the time.**

It means Bree can't work on the cabin and, with the first burst of urgency gone, that project seems like a dream.

Cleo and I collect maple sap a few times, but I couldn't say how many – only that all the storage containers we have are quite full. "I guess we need to boil this down soon," I say.

Cleo nods, "One of these days." The days-blending-together syndrome appears to have hit her, too.

There are a few notable things. I froze a huge batch of chili right before the pandemic hit, as my contribution to a potluck St. Patrick's Day dinner that was supposed to be held in the community hall.

It's been canceled.

I leave the chili on Bree and Charlie's front porch and text Bree. **Open your front door. That's your dinner for tonight.**

She texts back **I am literally crying. Thank you so much.**

One thing I am aware of is the background sense of guilt I carry around with me during those days. The guilt that Dob reached out to me, and I didn't even reply.

And, sure, I do stand by the argument that I was allowed some time to think, but at some point the guy deserves a response.

I keep expecting him to stick his head out of the loft door, or even wander down to the sand ring while I'm working with the horses. I figure he'll want to see Campbell's neck since he was part of that repair.

Every time I'm out and around and I don't see him I feel a mix of relief and dread. Is he more hurt than I thought? Is it going to be up to me to go knock on his door?

Finally, the decision gets made for me toward the end of the second ...? third ...? someday, anyway. I pull my sheets in from the clothesline and the wind's blown all the stiffness out of them and, when I carry the basket inside they smell like wind that's blown over the river, and the fields, and had sunlight filtered through it, and I realize it's time for me to give Dob fresh sheets.

I choose the top set from my "paying guests" pile – high thread count, good elastic in the fitted sheets, tasteful patterns – and put them in a laundry basket with a note: **If you have clothes you need washed, throw them in here and I'll do a load for you.**

On my way across the gravel of the yard I take a moment to notice I'm warm enough without a jacket and as I mount the stairs my head's busy with wondering how much longer our maple sap will run, and whether this is the year I should try to grow potatoes, and whether it's safe to finally wash all the horses' winter blankets ...

"Well, hey there."

"Whoa!" I take a step back, and Dob must be afraid I'm going to tumble down the stairs because he steps forward and reaches for me. "No! I'm fine. It's OK." I free up a hand to steady myself on the railing and thank goodness I rebuilt all the banisters before I started renting the loft out.

"You good?" The way he looks at me – I remember it – it's like I'm the only person in the world and whether I'm OK is the only thing he has room to think about. It's what he used to do when I'd come home venting about a kid who sat facing the wrong direction in class, or a parent who called the classroom and reamed me out about their child's bad grades before I could explain I was just the supply teacher.

He'd say, "Tell me about it," and give me that look, until I'd notice him sneaking sideways glances at his phone and I'd say, "You want to go meet Bob for a beer, don't you?" or "You have an ultimate game," and he'd grin and say, "Only if you're OK," and of course I'd say I was, because he'd already listened to me for a good five minutes.

"Yes," I say now. "Fine. A bit busy – I'm not sure where the days have gone – and I was meaning to mention that to you ..."

He runs his hand through his messy, floppy – undeniably very sexy – hair and says, "Yeah, about that. I'm really sorry."

"You're sorry ...?"

"I had such good intentions when I wrote that note ..." He inserts his winning grin, combined with his concerned look, "... then I came back here and had a beer and fell asleep, and by the time I woke up it was dark. I hope you weren't starving waiting for me."

"I, uh ..."

"And I've been meaning to make it up to you, but these last couple of days – it's a long story, but the guy who owns the outdoor guiding company I was working for in Yukon has an idea to expand his business, and he's had me on Zoom calls off and on. Anyway, I told him about this place, and ... well maybe you and I should talk about the opportunity while I finally make you that dinner I promised."

This is something I remember too. I'd forgotten it, actually, but it all comes back to me now. How I'd think something was about me – like when Dob would act all secretive in the days leading up to my birthday, and I'd give him space because he was probably planning a special evening for me, then I'd find out he'd really been hatching a plan with his buddies to pull together a boys' weekend at a progressive metal festival.

I thought I'd hurt his feelings by not responding to his dinner invitation.

He'd fallen asleep.

"Hey, Aspen, what do you think?"

I blink. I breathe. I channel everything I can into giving Dob one of his own charismatic smiles. "I promised Bree I'd finish up in the cabin so she can take over tomorrow."

"Ah!" He gives me a wink and a thumbs up. "Exactly why you'd be a good partner for this venture. High standards. Always improving. I like that."

"Yes, well, speaking of which," I thrust the laundry basket toward him. "Clean sheets. Sorry I can't put them on for you."

He lifts the basket to his nose. "Line dried? It's these little touches that make your place great, Aspen. Which reminds me, I'd like to stay until after Easter. It would be nice if we could celebrate it together. And about the business opportunity, I'll pull a bit more information together and we can circle back to this, OK?"

I mimic his wink and thumbs up, and feel like a great big fake, but he says, "Excellent. Go make that cabin even better!"

Back in the house I make another peanut butter and jam sandwich, whistle Pearson to my side, head back to the cabin, and since the painting's done I scrub the entire place, from dusting the top of the curtain rods, to getting on my hands and knees to wash the floor. It's not as much fun without John to talk to, but it would be harder for him to hear me anyway, as I whirlwind around the space.

When I'm done I snap a picture of the freshly painted, spotless, blank canvas of a living room and text it to Bree saying, **Clean as a whistle – ready when you are!**

It's time to take back my days. It's time to move forward.

Ten

So far, so good. The sun's still working its way above the horizon when I finish my run the next morning.

Taking back my days ...

I turn the horses out and tackle the barn, still in my running clothes.

It's amazing to have accomplished so much before breakfast. Inside, I switch the kettle on. While it boils, I turn on the radio and, for the first time in a long time, it's good to hear the news begin, "Good morning, today is Tuesday, March 24 ..."

Tuesday, I think. *Taking back my days.*

Yogurt in a bowl, with homemade granola, and a steaming mug beside me. Heaven. This is going to be a good day. I've decided it is.

My inbox has a picture from Agatha taken from her balcony in Mexico. **Missing the girls, but the twenty-five-degree weather helps make up for it!** That makes me smile.

There's also a notification that the Mason jars I ordered to bottle our maple syrup will be delivered today. Excellent.

I get a jump of excitement, and nerves when I open a message replying to my posting on the Island Help message board. Thank you for your posting about offering board for a couple of horses during the pandemic. I'm a nurse working at the assessment centre in the city. I have a mare in foal and a companion donkey and if you'd take them, I could move into my sister's place on the mainland which would make my life much easier while all this is going on. Could you tell me if that's possible?

There's a newsletter from the vacation rental site where I list the loft and the cabin. Why not take this time during the pandemic to improve your property? it suggests. Done that ... thanks to Bree.

My stomach tightens as I read the next message, from the township. Property taxes are officially deferred. Good news. But they're still owing, and collecting interest. *Shit.*

I blow out a long exhale and take a sip of my drink. Whatever. There's absolutely nothing I can do about it now. Other than improve my vacation rental property. Focus on the positive.

The final bolded message is from John. **Favour.**

Hi Aspen.

I have to say our conversation the other day was the highlight of my week. Since then my life has been all Zoom meetings full of unintentional mutings and people's cats walking over their keyboards, and lining up around the block for the privilege of entering the grocery store, and browsing the Old Navy pyjama section, because clearly I don't own enough elastic waist pants for the kind of work I'm doing these days.

Anyway, enough about me – I'm writing about somebody who's actually worthy of concern.

Do you remember my friend Scott, who you met when you were in town (that was fun, by the way) – Scott, the ER doctor? You might also remember me mentioning his wife was pregnant?

Well, she's had the baby – a very cute, healthy little girl – and Scott is worried sick about them. They live in a condo smaller than mine, and he's coming home from his shifts late at night, already exhausted, then spending all this extra time trying to peel off his clothes in the hallway (without the neighbours calling the police) and showering as soon as he gets in, but he's still terrified of bringing the virus home to Natalie and the baby.

The reason I'm mentioning this is that a few of us have put together a fundraising page and we've raised enough money to pay for Natalie and the baby to stay somewhere else for a while. When I thought of the safest, most relaxing, most amazing place in the world, I thought of your place, and I wondered if you'd be willing to rent the loft to them for the next month or so.

I'm asking you by email to let you think it over and decide with no pressure from me (no pressure!).

I know you have a lot of responsibilities, and this might be one too many, and if that's the case, I completely respect that.

Please let me know once you've decided.

Thinking of you,

John

I take Mocha on a long hack and I think about it the whole time.

I think I wouldn't be surprised at all to find out the entire "fundraising page" has been bankrolled by John.

"He's generous like that, isn't he Mocha?" I scratch her withers.

I think he knows, full well, how much I need money right now.

"Your mom's paying me, but not enough to run the whole place." Mocha flicks an ear to me, leaves the other one pitched forward toward the spot where a deer just bounded into the woods.

I think of what it would be like to have a young mom and her baby staying in the loft as the spring blooms, and Easter comes and goes and, maybe, as a foal is born on the farm.

We ride by the tall platform where the ospreys nest every year, as one of the adults swoops in clutching sticks in his talons.

I think of all the change that's been put in front of me this morning – new people, new horses – and there's a familiar uncertainty about it. What if I have to deliver a foal? What if the woman from the city hates it here?

I also experience the stirrings of the courage that's been growing in me. New foals used to be born on this farm every spring – even if I didn't deliver them, I have some experience. And all anyone wants these days is to feel safe. I can offer that to a woman and her baby.

The breeze lifts Mocha's mane and she gives a little jig. "Walk," I say, and as soon as she settles, I say, "Good girl – let's go!" and I don't know which one of us feels better as she jumps forward into a swinging trot.

***

A bite comes into the air as the day progresses and the noon news warns of overnight frost. I shrug – this is spring in Ontario; two steps forward, one step back – I add a down vest on top of my other layers when I take Abbott out to collect the sap.

He's become an old hand at this in the few days he's been doing it. I reckon he could give Sam a run for his money in identifying all the maples in the woodlot. I don't have to tell him when to stop anymore – he marches forward until the wagon's next to one of our tapped trees, then he halts.

Somebody would pay a lot of money for a horse as promising as this one. They'd love to have him at the Canadian heritage park where quite a few of my aunt's home-breds now pull visitors on wagon rides, or in the tow scow along the canal.

At the beginning of this pandemic the thought would have filled me with dread – *what if I have to sell him?* – now it's mostly pride. He's a great horse – partly by breeding and partly by training. I'm starting to be more confident I'll manage. I'll get through these times. I won't have to have a fire sale of my favourite things.

Cleo meets me close to the end of the trail. Abbott and I have collected a huge amount of sap today, but Cleo doesn't look happy about it.

"Oh, there's so much. I don't even know if all this will fit in the storage containers. Why did I think this was a good idea ...?"

"Cleo?"

"Yes?"

"Are you stressed?"

"My video is due tomorrow. I mean, of course, it's not that big a deal if I don't get it in, but I *want* to get it in – I *hate* submitting things late – and I didn't know how much sap there would be – I mean I *knew*, but it's different seeing it, and ..."

"What if I start boiling it down?"

"You?"

"Yes, me. You have the pans – right? You told me you got those old chafing pans the grill was going to get rid of."

She nods.

"So, if you can light the fire in the pit while I take Abbott home, it should be nice and hot by the time I come back and I can sit and read for a couple of hours while the sap boils."

The reading sounds like a great idea. I even bring my Kindle with a bunch of fresh books on it I haven't even launched yet.

But I don't read.

I think some more.

Then I make a conscious effort to stop thinking and feel instead. I sit quietly, one hand on the head of the dog I've become used to having by my side, listening to the occasional pops and hisses of the hot fire, holding my hands out to the heat thrown off by the white-hot embers, staring through the trees at the top of the embankment – just starting to have a green fuzz along their branches – letting me see right through to the grey of the river.

I feel a mixture of hope, resignation, happiness, regret, and some relief.

I match the feelings to the thoughts that generated them, then decide it's time to start acting, and piggyback on Bree and Charlie's Wi-Fi to send some emails.

As I'm finishing the first chapter of my first book, Bree lifts a main floor window to say she knows Bix is getting better because he's eaten the best part of a brick of ice cream – "I made him milkshakes, which he's trying to tell me are healthy because there are strawberries in them," – and it's a good thing she stocked up on toilet paper, because having everyone at home all the time is really increasing their consumption rate, and she's suddenly desperate to have her hair cut – "Which is dumb because I never get my hair cut, and it's not like I'm going to be seeing anybody who isn't already obliged to love me just the way I am, but there it is." She takes a deep breath. "How about you? What's new?"

I open my mouth, then close it again. "Not much, really," and, thankfully a much-happier-than-before Cleo comes running around the house to keep my friend-who-knows-me-too-well from asking more questions.

I'll tell her when everything is sorted out.

Eleven

A smoky scent with sweet undertones – sap, I'm guessing – clings to me as I walk home through the woodlot.

I'm doing sums in my head. How many gallons of sap we started with. How much more we'll likely collect. How much maple syrup it will boil into. How much money Cleo will end up with for her fundraiser.

Unfortunately, the final amount is modest to say the most.

Oh well. It's better than nothing. It's all about getting by, doing your best, staying positive. I just hope Cleo won't be disappointed.

"Aspen!"

I stop and turn. Cleo's belting through the woods toward me.

"What is it, Cleo? Don't tell me you forgot the final temperature for the syrup?"

She stops, ribs heaving. "No. Nothing to do with syrup." She pants a couple of times. "Well, not *making* syrup. It does have to do with the fundraising project we're making the syrup for."

"What do you mean?"

She narrows her eyes. "I think you might know exactly what I mean."

"I wish I did because you seem really excited by it."

"Your donation ..."

"Oh, gosh, Cleo. I'm sorry if I let you down. I didn't know the page was set up yet. I actually ..." I hunt around in the pocket of my vest. The last time I wore this was back when the world was accepting cash. "Yup! Look – can I give you cash? It's your lucky day – I don't often have two twenties in my pocket."

"Two twenties?"

"I did warn you it wouldn't be a huge donation."

"No. That's not it ... so, you're telling me you really don't know anything about it?"

"About what, Cleo?"

"The five-hundred-dollar donation I got."

"The what? How? Who? When?"

"Obviously I don't know who, because I thought it was you." She takes a deep breath. "I haven't logged onto my page for a couple of days because I was waiting until our 4H group chose a charity to support so I could change the page description from raising money for our trip to raising money for the specific charity – which, by the way, is going to be the Humane Society. So, anyway I logged in just now to make the update and there was this huge donation!"

"Doesn't it have a name attached to it?"

She lifts her palms to the sky. "Anonymous."

"You have no idea?"

"There's just a note that says "I hope this gets your fundraising off to a good start. Keep up the great work!" which is so weird because nobody knows we switched to fundraising. I mean, except my parents, who wouldn't have given me five hundred dollars, and you who – well, I didn't think you had five hundred dollars, but you're the only other person who knows.

"Yeah. That is so weird." The thing that's weird is how my voice sounds, because even as I'm replying to Cleo, I'm thinking of a certain person who knew Cleo was going to be fundraising.

He wouldn't ... but even as I'm thinking that, I know he would. In fact, it's the exact kind of thing he'd do.

I smile at Cleo. "I'm super happy for you. I wish I could hug you."

She laughs. "I don't need a hug. I got five hundred dollars!"

"Good point."

I walk the rest of the way home glad that Cleo came running out to tell me because it erases any tiny lingering doubts about all the decisions I made this afternoon.

When I come into the yard Pearson, who scampered ahead of me, is standing, feet braced, staring at Dob. Dob's saying, "For God's sake, dog. Ever since you saw her, you don't want anything to do with me."

Dob switches his gaze to me and says, "Although, I can't blame him. I never stopped thinking about you the whole time I was gone."

My afternoon of thinking and decision-making makes it easy to stop, and tilt my head and say, "That's such a weird thing to say."

"What do you mean?"

"You left me without any notice, or a backward glance, in the middle of our best friends' wedding, so if you've been thinking about me, it must have started quite a while after that." Pearson trots to my side and I scratch his ears.

Dob rubs his temples. "Clearly it's about time we talked. Do you have anything to barbecue? If so, I'll fire up the grill."

I open my mouth to protest his plan to make up to me by serving me my own food, then decide, what the heck – I do need to talk to him, and I do need to eat, so I might as well give him the job of standing in front of the barbecue.

***

The overnight frost is seeming more and more likely and, despite the fire, I'm already chilled from sitting outside at Bree and Charlie's all afternoon. There's no way I'm eating dinner outside.

I put a chair by the kitchen door, with a folding table next to it, then I set a spot for myself at the small kitchen table at the other end of the room.

"Really?" Dob asks when he sees it.

"Um, yeah."

"You do remember that I wasn't actually in the US, right? That was a ruse to get you to let me back into your life?"

"Just because you weren't in the States, doesn't mean you're safe." *And just because you're in my kitchen, doesn't mean you're back in my life.*

"But I was hoping ..."

I point to his chair. "Let's eat, then let's talk."

He rubs his stomach. "Yes. OK. Since I'm starving, I'll go along with that."

"Nice dinner."

"Thanks," Dob says. "I've learned to cook pretty well over the last few years."

I don't point out that I made the salad and boiled the corn. "Good for you."

"It could also be good for you."

Here we go. He leans forward and I become acutely aware of how the only thing separating us is two metres of empty space, and the requests of public health officials, and our own willingness to cooperate.

It's been years since Dob touched me. Months since I touched any other man. Over a week since I've even touched another human being.

It might have been years, but I know exactly how it would go. How Dob would run his hand up the back of my head, and spread his fingers through my hair. How we'd move all around the kitchen – he'd lift me to the counter and push his way between my legs, he'd sit in a kitchen chair and pull me into his lap, he'd open the fridge and find whipped cream, or chocolate syrup – maple syrup would do in a pinch.

Dob loved athletic sex and props. He loved spontaneity and creativity.

"You're thinking about it, aren't you?" he says.

"Thinking about what?"

"About how it's time for dessert and how we could find a fun way to share the last of my Double Stuf Oreos."

I smile. "I see you haven't changed." It's true that his sharp cheekbones, and square shoulders, and lean hips all look the same, and I can imagine how each part of him would feel under my hands. I wonder what he has in mind for those Double Stuf Oreos ...

He shifts in his chair and says, "In some important ways, I haven't changed, and in some other ways, I really have."

This is the part I've spent years longing for, imagining, wanting. For Dob to make everything better. To heal the hurt and say it'll never happen again, and to make me believe it.

Except ... now I've found a way to believe it for myself.

It's so tempting to say, *"Tell me how you've changed ..."* To hear him explain. To let him make promises. To bring all my daydreams to life.

Instead I say, "We need to talk."

He gives the dead-sexy, lazy, lopsided grin that could always hook me, and says, "I agree. And you know the best way to talk."

It makes me laugh out loud because, for Dob, that was always naked. I'd ask, "Should I teach summer school?" or "Should we find a new apartment when our lease comes up?" or "How about going on a trip together after Bree and Charlie's wedding?" and he'd nibble on my ear, and slide his hand up my shirt and say, "That is something I'd like to discuss very seriously, right after we do this, first ..."

He stands up, and says, "Yes, then?"

I push my chair back a foot.

He takes a step forward.

I scramble up and behind the chair.

This space – this magical two metres which has become both practical and symbolic over the last little while; represented on signs, by arrows, by people holding metre sticks, by a man roaming the streets of Toronto in a sphere made out of children's connector sticks, showing precisely how far two metres is – it's like a forcefield between Dob and me.

If I can just keep it between us, I'll be fine.

He advances, I fall back.

"Aspen," he says.

"What?" It's a whisper.

"Are you going to keep backing up?" He holds his hands out. They're now definitely closer to me than two metres. "Please don't. Everything good that we had before – it's still there. And all the bad stuff – I've learned, and I'll listen, and I'll never, ever do anything like that to you again."

A wall I didn't even know was there breaks in me. It brings tears welling to my eyes. It thickens my voice.

"Oh, Dob," I say. "That is the exact perfect thing to say." I sniff. I blink. "And I'm going to have to ask you to move out."

Twelve

He hasn't changed that much.

I'd forgotten that he used to sulk. He reminds me the next morning, though, with every pointed side glance as he loads his car. With every too-loud slam of the hatch, and with every sigh whenever I'm in earshot.

After one sigh so loud I can hear it as I turn Lemon out, I put on the sweetest smile I can muster. "Is there anything I can help you with?"

"No. Thank. You."

"Alright then. If there is, just let me know."

It's not a fatal flaw. It wasn't the thing that bugged me the most about him way back when. In fact, if he hadn't left me at somebody else's altar, it would have hardly been a blot on our relationship.

But given that he did do that, and we're not together anymore, it's a distinctly unattractive trait. If he thinks it's going to make me sorry that I asked him to leave, it's having quite the opposite effect.

To be fair, I'm probably getting on his nerves with my shiny eyes, and bright smile, as I bop through my morning humming Arkell's "My Heart's Always Yours."

I expected to be wracked with guilt. To toss and turn all night. To be full of remorse and second thoughts.

Instead I put my head on the pillow and opened my eyes eight hours later, rested to the core.

I replied to John's email saying I'd be delighted to have Natalie to stay. Give me a call when you have a chance.

Then I came out to the yard where the stalls were unusually clean, and Lemon didn't put a foot wrong during her dressage school.

Now, feeling full of reckless happiness, I text Bree. It's been ages since we rode together. If Bix is well enough for you to leave him, why don't we take Campbell and Mocha on a hack?

Ever so briefly, as I figure-eight Lemon's bridle, I think it's funny John hasn't called yet. Then I think, no – of course it isn't – he's very busy, and just because he isn't going into the office doesn't mean he doesn't have wall-to-wall Zoom meetings and phone calls, and I'm sure he'll call soon.

I also remember it's completely like me to leave my phone on silent when I'm waiting for a call, and I pull it out of my pocket to check the ringer.

I'm shoving the wheelbarrow up the side of the manure pile when my phone pings. I lose hold of one handle, and the whole thing tilts to one side, while I tumble to the other.

Lying in the dung, I wriggle my phone out of my back pocket to find a message from Bree. **Yes! What a great idea! Charlie's going to watch the latest Star Wars movie with Bix while I come with you. First thing after lunch?**

Excellent, I tell myself. **Excellent.** I reply. That's exactly the message I wanted.

"Important message?" Dob's standing, arms crossed and feet wide, by the bottom of the loft stairs.

I struggle to regain that feeling of calm, smug superiority I felt a few short minutes ago. Back when I thought Dob needed to suck it up, and I felt bulletproof.

There are soiled shavings in my pocket, though. And in my hair. And some might have worked their way into my bra. And there's doubt in my heart. Just a tiny bit.

Because of course John is the best person in the world. And of course he's going to call me back. And of course this is all going to work out.

Except ... it's unusual for him not to have at least sent me a quick text saying, **In meetings now. Will call later.** Or something.

I stand up and brush myself down, and Dob whistles "My Heart's Always Yours", and the mockery of it short-circuits all my good sense and I whirl around and stick my tongue out at him.

"Whoa!" He throws his hands up. "Did you stick your tongue out at me?"

I wrinkle my nose and give him the middle finger.

"Wow. From strength to strength."

"Oh ... you ..." I clench my fists and stride toward him, and he puts his hands in the air and starts backing up.

"Oh, no-no-no," he says. "Remember. Two metres."

I quicken my pace and raise my fists. "You didn't care about two metres last night."

He backs toward the row of stones separating the grass from the gravel. "But you were right, and I was wrong. Two metres is very important."

I take a step. "You ..." *step*, "... are ..." *step* "... completely ..." *step* "... infuriating ..." *step* "And you've still ..." *step* "never apologized ..." *step* "... for what you did ..."

For each step I take forward, he takes one back, until he takes the final step that puts him onto the gravel, then he's dancing. "Ow! Ow! Ow!" and I'm yelling, "For the love of God, that's what you get for not wearing shoes – what kind of idiot goes barefoot around a barn?" and he's yelling, "I didn't have any intention of being in the barn!" and I say, "That's you all over, Dob – you don't think, you never have any intentions, you just do what you want to in the second you want to do it!"

He's leaping from one foot to the other on the sharp gravel and I'm yelling at him from behind my raised fists, and Bree, walking up the driveway, yells, "What the hell is going on here?"

***

Bree and I ride all the way to the end of the driveway, and turn right onto the road, before she says, "So?"

"So, what?"

"So, what on earth was that ridiculous display I walked in on?"

It's one of those moments when I want Bree to know everything that's happened while she was cooped up in her house with Bix, but I don't want to have to tell her, and I'm far too overwhelmed to figure out where to start, so I try to hone in on the most important, main thing and I finally say, "I'm in love with John."

"Oh!" she says. "Come here!"

"What?"

"I mean just stand there. Make Mocha stand." Then because Campbell is the sweetest, loveliest, best-trained mare in the world, she lets Bree sidle her right up to Mocha and stands perfectly still while Bree leans over and hugs me, and mumbles through my hair, "I'm sorry if what Bix had was the virus, and I'm giving it to you by hugging you, but if you die, at least we can all say you came to your senses before the end of your life."

"So you think John is the right person for me to be in love with?"

"I think John is the person you should marry and have six children with."

"I'm not sure I want six children."

"Well, you don't have to start on that right away but you do have to tell me how this happened."

We get the mares walking forward again, and I tell her. "Dob came back."

She nods. "I did know that part."

"And I was afraid to admit this to you, but I always had this daydream, or idea, or feeling, or ... whatever, that he'd come back and he'd have some good explanation, and he'd apologize, and we could ..."

"... live happily ever after?" Bree says.

I lift my eyebrows at her and she says, "As if I didn't know that's what you wanted, and it's why you passed up perfectly nice people, like that guy from my yoga instruction class I introduced you to."

"Bree! He only ate food that had been put through a blender first!"

"That's because he had a digestive condition – it wasn't his fault."

I lift my eyebrows higher.

"OK, OK – he might not have been the perfect candidate. But, John ..."

"Yes, well, I admit John is the perfect candidate and, if you recall, I did sleep with him, and I've just told you I'm in love with him, so what's the problem?"

"The problem is, you would never have seen him again if he hadn't called and offered to renovate your entire falling-down cabin for free, and even after that, you kept putting him off. He would have come here every weekend if you'd asked him, and he invited you to Toronto so many times, and you only went when there were horse events happening."

"It's not that simple ..." I spool back through all my excuses. Of how I had the horses to take care of. Of how I could get a supply teaching call in the very early hours of Monday morning – or even Sunday night. Of how I could be in Toronto, or John could be here, and that could be the very moment Dob showed up – that thought had definitely been there as well.

I think of how I've been waiting all morning for John to acknowledge my message.

"Do you think I screwed up?"

"No! Absolutely not!" I love her certainty. I love it less when she adds, "Unless there's something I don't know. You didn't tell him Dob was here, did you?" She sucks her breath in. "John didn't drive up here and find your ex-boyfriend weathering the pandemic on your property, did he?"

"No! Nothing like that."

"Why don't you go back to where you started and tell me everything?"

I lean forward and run my hand down Mocha's neck, sink my heels deeper, roll my shoulders back, and say, "OK, as I was saying, Dob showed up ..."

We ride along, past fields just starting to green, past trees just starting to bud, past a herd of cows with a couple of early-season calves in their midst, and I explain how I kept waiting for it to feel like a dream come true, that Dob had come home, and it didn't.

"And I thought maybe it was me – that this pandemic had me off-kilter and the worry meant I couldn't be happy, but lots of little things made me happy, like every single thing about Cleo, and how great Abbott's been, then the other night when I was putting the second coat on the cabin ..."

"Which, by the way, looks very good," Bree interrupts.

"Thank you – anyway, I talked to John on the phone the whole time I was painting and it was so ..."

"... nice?"

I nod. "Nice, but not in a boring way."

"You've just described my marriage," Bree tells me.

"Lucky."

"You could be lucky, too."

"Could I?" I pat my pocket with my phone in it. "He still hasn't called."

"Tell me the rest."

I explain about the Go Fund Me for his friend's wife – "Except I'm sure it's mostly John, just like it was him who donated the five hundred dollars to Cleo's page."

"That was John?"

"I told him about it the other night ..."

"... and you and Charlie and I were the only other people who knew, and we didn't do it ..."

"Exactly."

"Oh, God, Aspen. Marry him."

"I'd like him to call first."

"So, what's this call about?"

"I said it's to discuss details of Natalie coming here, but I'm also, thinking ... no, I've decided ... I mean, I'm almost sure ..."

"You're going to ask him to marry you!" The squeal in Bree's voice makes even sweet-and-reliable Campbell lift her head and prick her ears, and Mocha does a sideways jig under me.

"I'm going to ask him to move here for the rest of the lockdown."

"Oh! A close second to a marriage proposal. But, wait, with all these extra people moving to your property, what about Dob?"

"Remember you asked what the hell was going on when you arrived? That was the fallout from me telling Dob he needs to move out."

She grins. "I love it!"

**

The last thing Bree says to me before she heads home after our ride is, "Remember, John doesn't know his life will change when he returns your call. He might call faster if he did."

Fair enough. She's probably right. But for the first time ever it's me waiting for him to call, instead of the other way around.

It's gut-twisting.

I wonder if I made him feel this way.

I'm sorry.

"I'm sorry."

I turn from the gate, where I've let the two mares go, to face Dob.

"I've been really immature," he says. "It's that, I've had this daydream, for years now, of how one day it would be the right time for me to come back here, and when I did, we'd move forward again. Then the pandemic came, and

the lockdown, and I thought, 'This is it. This is the time.'"
He shakes his head. "It probably sounds stupid."

I smile. "Not stupid. I get it. I had that same daydream."

"But, no ..."

"But no." I pause. "Are you going to move to Cindy's?" It was one of the emails I sent yesterday – to a woman I know who also rents out a couple of cabins at the other end of the island. We help each other out when we can – take overflow guests. She'd replied almost instantly to say she could use the business and would be happy to put Dob up if he wants to go.

He nods. "For the next little while. After that ... I'm not sure. I do believe there's something to the idea that this pandemic makes you want to come home, but I don't know if I was coming here because I thought this place was home, or because I thought you were."

"Yeah, I ..."

My phone rings. I freeze. My heart jumps and my pulse flutters. I can barely breathe. I look at Dob. "I have to take this."

He nods. "Of course."

I put the phone to my ear. "Hi."

"Hi," John says.

My whole body relaxes. It feels like coming home.

***

I walk to the cabin while we discuss the details of Natalie's arrival. "I'll let you two talk it over," John says. "But it'll take her a couple of days to get organized. There's a lot to bring with a new baby."

"That's perfect." I plan it out. I can let the loft sit for a while on the very off chance there's any virus there, then get in and give it a good clean. "I'll make sure it's safe and sound for her when she gets here."

"This is great, Aspen. I can't think of a better place to be in this crazy time."

"Speaking of which ..." I climb the stairs to the cabin porch, lean out over the railing and watch a raft of geese skim across the surface of the bay.

"Speaking of which, what?"

"Speaking of which," I press my hand to my chest, feel the hammer of my heart. *Say it fast. Spit it out. The worst he can say is no.* "Since you don't have to go into the office anymore, I was wondering if you'd be able to ... I mean, if you'd like to ... I mean, if you would – I was wondering about you coming here. For the rest of the lockdown." Because he hasn't interrupted me, I keep talking. Or, possibly, babbling. "To stay with me. In my house. I have decent internet, and food in my freezer, and lots of toilet paper."

"We don't need toilet paper."

"We might need toilet paper."

"What I'm trying to say is I'd come even if you didn't have the toilet paper."

"So the internet and the freezer meals are enough?"

"Aspen?"

"Yes?"

"Are you serious?"

"Yes."

"Are you sure?"

"Absolutely."

"Aspen?"

"Yes?"

"I would have called you back so much earlier if I'd known you were going to ask me this."

Thirteen

Just like Dob, John arrives in the dark, but this time I'm wide awake. Nervous and jittery.

He texted me from the ferry dock, so I've timed night check for when he pulls up the driveway.

The barn is clean, secure, and cozy. Our new boarders arrived earlier today. The mare has a soft eye and a distinctly foal-shaped bulge in her belly. She, and the existing four horses fill all the full-sized box stalls with the donkey in the pony stall next to the tack room.

I shut out the lights and stand in the doorway with the rustling sounds of comfortable horses behind me, and Pearson by my side.

Dob told me the dog's story right before he left. That one day, he was cross-country skiing at the edge of town when a guy came up on a snowmobile. He had the dog on a long rope. He handed the rope to Dob, said, "Here, hold him for a minute, would you?" and accelerated away.

Dob never saw him again.

"I feel like a failure," Dob told me. "That dog was my responsibility, and I couldn't even get him to like me. I didn't even give him a name."

"You brought him here," I said. "Maybe that was your part in the bigger picture."

Now Pearson shifts. His ears cock forward. To me the night is nothing but a big windswept expanse. The sky is immense and emblazoned with star spray. As I watch, the dark bulk of a cloud scuds over the moon, then moves on.

And there it is. Down the quiet road. Light. From the car Pearson heard a long minute ago.

The car slows and swings onto my driveway, and the light resolves into two beams.

John.

"Stay close," I tell Pearson, and together we step forward into the yard.

* * *

After five minutes of awkwardness – "How was the drive?" and "How have you been?" and "He's a nice dog, isn't he?" and each of us staying two metres from the other because it's become a habit so quickly; replacing the old, more intimate ones of shaking hands or giving a quick hug, I say, "Screw it. Leave your stuff here and come upstairs."

Then I add, "I mean, please. I mean, if you want to."

He laughs. "I want to."

When we get to my bedroom – fresh-smelling because the bed's made up with line-dried sheets, and I left the window open most of the day to let the room fill with the scents of the fields and the river – John says, "Can I tell you how happy I am that you invited me here?"

I shake my head, take one deliberate step to break the two-metre bubble, take another to press myself up against the front of him, and whisper in his ear, "No. You need to show me."

He does.

With a slow dance around the room, that turns into a sway. His hands spreading across my back, moving up to span my ribs, his thumbs reaching to brush my nipples. Even through my shirt his touch makes me gasp.

It also makes me determined to get my shirt off.

He helps me with that, reaching down for the hem, yanking it over my head, kissing me through the thin fabric when it gets caught over my face. I start by laughing and end by moaning as we finally get it pulled over my head and we're kissing, lips touching, my skin alive to every place he touches it, my core aching to have him closer.

"I want you," I say.

He backs me up against the bed and I fall back onto it. With both of us working on my jeans, they're off in a minute, then with him standing at the end of the bed, we turn to removing his. I sit up, put my arms around him, press my cheek against his body – warm and tight – and I mumble, "The boxer shorts have got to go."

There's a moment when he's in me, when I have my legs wrapped around his waist, when our faces are pressed together and I can feel the faintest stubble against my skin, that I say, "This is perfect."

It is. It's intense and gentle. It takes just the right amount of time. As I clench my fist and thrust my whole body up from the mattress to press against him, and the waves of my orgasm wash through me I'm completely satisfied ... and I'm going to want more before too long.

"Thanks for coming," I say. Then giggle.

"Thanks for having me." He giggles, too.

"Let's do this again in the morning." Those words are the very last thing I remember before I open my eyes at 7:00 a.m. on a brand-new day.

Fourteen

Bree: Remember, it's an adjustment for both of you.

Me: OK. Will remember.

Bree: Seriously, Aspen. Even though Charlie and I had been together forever — had a daughter together — it took a while to get used to living together.

Me: It's fine. Really.

Bree: It will be better than fine.

Me: It *is* better than fine. It's perfect, and the sex is heavenly.

Bree: Why didn't you just say so?

Me: I didn't want to make you jealous, since you're an old, married woman and all.

Bree: If I didn't love you, I'd have to kill you.

"What are you laughing at?" John comes into the kitchen, barefoot, in t-shirt and boxers with his hair mussed. Funny, his bare feet don't bug me at all.

I hand him my phone.

"Heavenly?"

"I couldn't decide between that and 'scrumptious,' but I thought that made you sound like a coconut cream pie."

"I'll take heavenly."

I slide my hands around his waist, *"I'll take heavenly ..."*

***

Natalie arrives on the 1:00 ferry with her baby red-faced and screaming in the car seat. "Go straight up to the loft and feed her. John and I will unload the car and put everything inside the door for you."

I'm placing the last bag down when Natalie says, "Aspen?"

I look in to see her sitting in the big armchair I placed in front of one of the dormer windows. "Yes?"

"I can't believe how beautiful this place is. I'm really happy to be here."

"Well, John made it happen, and I'm also very glad you're here."

I start to back out, when she says, "Aspen?"

"Yes?"

"Is this OK?"

She looks toward the ground where Pearson's nose is resting on her foot.

"Oh my goodness, I'm sorry. I'll call him out of there."

"No! Really. I love dogs. Our condo in Toronto is too small, but it's wonderful to have him here, as long as you don't mind."

"It's fine with me. As long as you tell me if he's being a pest."

I head back down the stairs remembering how wise I felt when I told Dob he was probably just Pearson's vessel to me. I'm not sure how I'm going to feel if it turns out I was just his vessel to Natalie.

***

We fall into a rhythm – John and me, and Natalie and her baby, and Pearson and the horses, and all of us together.

The nights stop dropping below zero and the buds are going to break on the trees any day, so Cleo and I remove the taps from our trees, and boil and can the last of our syrup. It's a divine colour, and tastes equally good, and even though I tell her not to worry – I'll supply it as part of her rent, Natalie buys a dozen Mason jars' worth. "To send back to Scott," she winks.

Agatha messages me to say she thinks endurance rides might go ahead even if events don't. I message her back to say I won't let up on Lemon and Mocha's conditioning.

John works from a desk we've set up in the living room. While Cleo and I teach Abbott to pull a harrow –

which has the side-effect of creating a vegetable garden I'm not sure I have time to tend to – I can glance in the window and see him frowning at his monitor, or pacing the room wearing a headset, or just looking out at us.

Hi, I mouth.

Hi, he mouths back.

"Ugh," Cleo says, and pretends to retch in the bushes.

After John's done work – or whenever he's ready for a break – Campbell and I teach him to ride. I never thought I wanted to give riding lessons – had no desire to repeat, "heels down," and "thumbs up" every twenty seconds. But Campbell's a willing and patient teacher, and John's a quick learner, and I don't mind it after all. Maybe it's something to think about in the future. There are so many things to think about in the future.

Another reason the riding lessons are worthwhile is that I decide John's good enough to go on a hack after a week or so.

We head out on the warmest day of the year so far – sunny, and breezy, with everything greening so quickly it seems to be happening as we watch.

Campbell's mane blows to the side and John touches her neck lightly. Although she's shed a lot of the winter coat that made the shaved area really stand out, and even though – with Cleo's help – I snipped the sutures out, the line of the injury is still quite visible. "What happened?"

I think of telling him part of the truth, then I think better of it. I tell him everything. How I stitched Campbell up, who helped me, why he was here.

When I'm done the first thing John says is, "You really stitched her up all by yourself? That's brave."

"Thank you. That means a lot. I haven't always felt brave, but I'm getting better." I twirl a piece of Lemon's mane. "What about the rest?"

John squints his eye against the sun as he turns to me. "I kind of knew."

"You did? How?"

"I could tell there was something holding you back."

"How did you know?"

"This is going to sound cheesy."

I laugh. "Tell me! Cheesy things are fun!"

He runs his hand down Campbell's neck. "Well, as soon as you figured out I wasn't gay ..."

"Ooh, yikes. My bad. I'm really glad you're not gay, by the way ..."

"Hmm, yes ... me too."

Lemon dances sideways, and I dance her back. "On with the cheesy story."

"That week in July ..."

"Yes?"

"It ... it changed my life, Aspen. See – sorry – cheesy. It was everything I wanted in one package. This gorgeous place, and working on the cabin – using my hands – and you … I didn't think I could be imagining the chemistry, and we had so much fun together, and it was like a dream, and if you'd asked me, I would have stayed. Quit my job. Left my stuff in the city, and lived here. With you."

"But I didn't."

"You didn't. And, of course, half the time I told myself it was me – you didn't like me enough – I was more into you than you were into me. But the other half of the time I thought – or at least I really hoped – there was something else you were dealing with."

"You're not upset?"

"I'm really relieved."

"Oh." I let Lemon sway my hips for a few strides, while I absorb this new feeling invading me. It might also be relief. "Halt her."

I don't have to say it again. Campbell is so well voice trained she stops square on the spot.

I coax Lemon sideways one step, then another. The dressage training I've given her is battling with her instinct not to stay in one spot, not to sidle up so closely to another horse. Since I know I won't have long, I lean over, curl my hand around John's neck, pull him over and, tilting my head to keep our helmets from clashing, kiss him hard on the lips.

Lemon pulls away, but I'm shot through with happiness, so it doesn't really matter.

"Does that mean you've sorted out what's holding you back?" John asks.

"I'd say it does."

***

Time moves forward as it always does on the island, with something special every day. One day it's Cleo and me spotting a merganser duck with sixteen ducklings as we're hacking Mocha and Lemon through the fields. Another day it's Abbott's first time being backed – with Cleo lying across his saddle while I lead him around the sand ring.

On Easter it's a big meal around the bonfire, with one chair for Natalie at twelve o'clock, two chairs for John and me at three, and a cluster of chairs for Bree, Charlie, Bix, and Cleo stretching between six and nine o'clock.

Pearson trots from chair to chair and Bree asks, "Is that dog ever going to decide who he belongs to?"

"He just follows the love," I say.

At which point she stands on the arms of her Muskoka chair, lifts her wineglass high and says, "To my best friend, Aspen, who has finally figured out how to follow the love – even if she had to learn it from a dog."

***

Easter Monday John and I walk through the already-growing grasses to the cabin.

Bree and I took pictures last week, and John helped me load them on the vacation rental site, and I've already snagged two bookings for next year at my significantly increased prices.

There's rain pressing in – not every day can be perfect on the island – but the grey skies and spatter of drops on the windows make the cabin even cozier.

Even though the furniture's the same, Bree's re-arranged it to frame the view. That, along with new curtains, whimsical wall art, and some bright cushions, make the interior look every bit as high-end as my vacation rental description now says it is.

"I can't believe the difference," John holds up his phone displaying the before picture I sent when I started painting. "Here, stand next to me and we'll take an 'after' selfie."

He snaps the photo and shows it to me – the two of us grinning madly in a room that looks like it could be in a magazine.

Before and after. There you have it.

I sink onto the couch, put my feet up on the ottoman, and pat the seat beside me. "Come look at the view with me."

We sit in a stretch of silence while swallows swoop and dip through the crazy air currents being created by the incoming weather. Is it fair to be this happy when so many people are having such a tough time?

It's just one of the many questions, and thoughts, and developments, and changes this pandemic has brought. I suppose there's comfort in the fact that some of the changes are positive.

"I have a question for you." John and I say it at the same time.

"You first," I say.

"OK. Have you ever thought of living here, instead of up at the house?"

I smile. "That kind of piggybacks on my question."

"How's that?"

"Bree thinks you want to be Premier one day. Do you?"

He shifts beside me. "I think I answered that the other day."

"You mean when you said working with your hands, on this cabin, was one of the happiest things you've ever done?"

"Mmm-hmm. And when I said I'd stay here forever if I could."

"So, not Premier?"

"Not unless I have to be."

I lean in, nudge my nose under his ear and whisper, "I'm not going to make you."

PLEASE LEAVE A REVIEW!

REVIEWS help me sell books. More sales let me write more books. A simple star rating and a few quick words are all that's needed to help other readers decide if they want to read my books.

To review, please follow this link – https://tinyurl.com/reviewBA – and select your preferred retailer. Or, use this QR code:

If you liked this book ...

... you might enjoy Tudor's other books. Read the first chapter of *In Search Of*, co-written with Mara Dabrishus, to find out.

In Search Of

Chapter One • Cam

There were so many things that could go wrong. Coming into something like this you had to tell yourself you were covering them off; all the possible roadblocks, disasters, obstacles. You had to believe that's what all the preparation was for.

But I knew as well as anyone else what a joke that was.

I could seize up. But, for me, that always happens on the bike, right after the swim. When my calf muscles have to transition right-quick from icy water and constant contraction to the flexing extension required for pedaling, while adjusting to the relative warmth of the air.

And here I was in the run with my muscles sliding along just fine.

I could chafe. It seems small but it's nothing to scoff at. A seam, a lace, a thread, a hair in the wrong place, and the burning and bleeding could make me lose – if not the will to live – then definitely the will to finish this race.

So far so good, though. Socks, shorts, shirt staying where they should. A nice breeze wicking the sweat from my exposed skin.

I could crash. But, again, the bike was the most likely place for that where too many riders – nerve-riddled and adrenaline-spiked – converged on narrow, twisting, hilly, potholed roads.

Over halfway through the run the field had straggled out. I ran through dappled shade and flickering sun in my own running space. A trip-up from another runner seemed unlikely.

Of course, for me, with my particular goal of an age-group win, there would always be the possibility of the other guys just being flat-out better.

I figured, coming in, there were half-a-dozen to really worry about. I'd already passed four of them.

At kilometre fourteen I had my eyes fixed on number five, and it was a particular pleasure to put a lock on his lycra-clad buttocks and reel him in.

I did it the way my swim coach taught me to move through the pool – pretending the water is something I can dig my arm into and pull my weight forward – I remembered that, and used this guy's sinewy hind end as my anchor, my reference point; propelling myself past him.

Fifteen strides to go until I passed the guy from Boston. How did I know he was from Boston? Everyone in the bar last night knew where he was from, as we spent what was supposed to be a relaxing evening listening to minute-by-minute details of his training routine, the cost of every single piece of equipment he'd brought with him, and everything he'd eaten for the last seventy-two hours, all in a fortissimo Boston accent.

Ten strides to go and I could picture the shock on the waitress's face as he casually reached out to pinch her ass when she brought him the bill.

Five strides to go and I re-lived the satisfaction of telling him to keep his hands to himself ... which led to the even more satisfying memory of how the waitress thanked me, back at her place, our bodies pressed hard against the front door, slamming it open, then again on the kitchen counter while we got side-tracked in our search for a drink, and finally using up all the hot water in her barely big-enough shower.

And still to bed in time for my seven hours of pre-Ironman sleep, leaving me fit and rested to beat the Boston blowhard.

In the final stride before I passed him, my hand hovered right behind his haunches and it took every bit of restraint in me not to pinch.

Hot sweaty man, I reminded myself, and pulled my hand in, hunkered down, and sailed past him.

The rest of the field down, one more to go.

By now I was pretty sure I wasn't going to hit the wall, either. I had six months of training to thank for that. So many, many weekends without beer and without the corresponding morning-after-the-night-before greasy breakfasts to sop up the hangovers.

Brick workouts, using up most of my weekends and leaving my then-girlfriend moaning, "Again? Do you really need to cycle to Kingston today?"

"Yes," I'd said every time.

"This isn't working," she'd said.

Oh, yes it is, I'd thought, while saying, "I'm really sorry, but there's no point in going into an Ironman unprepared."

And today's smooth swim, effortless cycle, and limber running legs were the result.

Maybe this training thing could be a permanent way of life after all.

I accelerated, just for fun, and it was easy – my lungs and legs shifted seamlessly to their new gear. In the far distance I spied a speck I hadn't seen before. Could that be guy number one in my age group? The last guy I had to catch?

Only one way to find out – keep running.

Maybe I could meet a woman who also liked to train. Who would be fast, strong, and wouldn't bug me. Who wouldn't make me resort to working out as a creative way to escape her.

The thought seemed so reasonable that I started scoping out the runners around me. All shapes and sizes … nothing illustrated that better than a triathlon. Stocky, stringy, wobbly – all were represented. Sweaty, scruffy, running-catalogue chic – I saw all those, too.

There was a woman off to my right, running with easy strides through the pure, clean Adirondack autumn sunshine. She had a long French braid – not perfect; that would be bizarre this far into a race – but something about its heaviness, the way it swung in a rope down her back, and the suggestion of the thickness of the hair it restrained, was very sexy.

Her legs were long, muscled, and tanned in a training-outdoors rather than a tanning-bed kind of way.

She glanced at me, and I tossed her a smile, and I thought, It's not that I can't commit. It's not that I'm a womanizer. It's that I haven't met the right woman, and maybe this is her …

"Stop!"

The girl blocking my way was all wrong.

The hand she held up sported nails so long they scared me, coated in a shade of glossy pink that hurt my eyes.

Her tan ... well it was not outdoor-natural.

And her hair – not much natural about that either.

Not to say I'd kick her out of bed, but I couldn't imagine ending up there with her in the first place, given the resentment I was feeling at her breaking my amazing running rhythm to allow the organic, athletic, all-natural, newly discovered soulmate and mother-of-my-future-children to pull steadily away from me.

"What is wrong with you?!?" I deked sideways, but her reflexes weren't half-bad; she jumped just as quickly, staying right in front of me, and saying, "There's nothing wrong with me ... it's him!" She pointed to a guy sprawled on the ground. While I watched he groaned and pulled himself into the fetal position. His knee was bleeding and so was his elbow.

OK, truth. I was not a very nice person. I wasn't selfless. I wanted what I wanted and I'd already decided I wanted an age-group win. Which, let's face it, was not going to happen if I stayed in this spot any longer.

But ... race karma.

No runner left behind.

It's a thing, both spoken, and unspoken. No single race result is more important than another person's well-being.

I knew it … I just couldn't feel it.

But if I kept running, and came first, there would be a dirty film over my win. An asterisk next to my result. He's the guy who left someone in pain / in distress / in trouble just so he could get a trophy. Who does that?

I wanted to do that.

The guy groaned again and rocked his body.

"Do something!" the girl yelled. "Help him!"

I'd like to say that's what changed my mind. I'd like to claim my concern for this guy, and my desire to step in and assist this Good-Samaritan girl, is what made me decide to stop.

In reality, loud-mouthed, obnoxious Boston-Guy pounded by me and I thought, I don't know if I have it in me to chase him down again, and there was no way I wanted him to beat me legitimately, so I sighed and met the girl's eyes for the first time, and said, "What, exactly, do you want me to do?"

If you liked the first chapter of In Search Of, why not read the rest of the book? You can find it using this QR code.

ABOUT THE AUTHOR

TUDOR ROBINS is the author of books that move your heart, mind, and pulse.

A little piece of Tudor's own heart is in many places: the central-Ottawa neighborhood where she lives, the Gatineau hills and Eastern Ontario countryside where she loves to hike, Wolfe Island and the St. Lawrence River where she loves swimming and paddleboarding, and the university towns that are currently home to her children.

When she's not writing, Tudor rides, runs, quilts, and walks with her best friends and her Jack Russell / Potcake mix, Cara.

Please contact Tudor at tudorrobins@gmail.com!

www.ingramcontent.com/pod-product-compliance
Lightning Source LLC
Chambersburg PA
CBHW031509120626
46545CB00005B/1797